101 secrets of imparting positivity to your teen

VIDYASHANKAR GURU

Clever Fox® PUBLISHING

Chennai • Bangalore

CLEVER FOX PUBLISHING
Chennai, India

Published by CLEVER FOX PUBLISHING 2025

PAPERBACK ISBN: 978-93-6707-493-0
HARDBACK ISBN: 978-93-6707-236-3

TABLE OF CONTENTS

INTRODUCTION

Today, parents of teenagers face numerous challenges, broadly classified into four major areas: capability, focus, academics, and negativity. However, perhaps the biggest obstacle is not capability itself; it's the pervasive negativity that influences their children. Ask yourself, *Is my child capable?* For many, the answer is likely "Yes, completely agree" or "Agree to some extent." Yet, contrary to common belief, the real issue lies not in a child's inherent abilities and capabilities but in the negativity they encounter.

No child is born with a negative attitude; rather, Negativity accumulates from their environment, including family dynamics, societal expectations, social pressures, academic pressure, lack of focus and concentration, family expectations & relationship problems. Out of all these issues, mobile addiction is a major one, often distracting them from studies and real-life connections. Peer pressure is another big factor, pushing teens to make choices based on what others think rather than what's right for them. The impact of the pandemic also lingers, making it hard for some to handle anxiety and stay positive. These issues create a lot of negativity, affecting both teens and their parents.

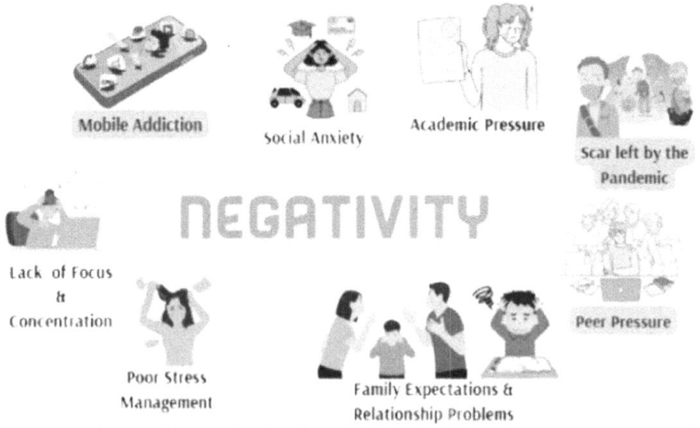

Negativity translates into many problems that affect a child's emotional well-being, academic success, and even family relationships. Many parents express concerns like, *My child can't concentrate, My child has a poor memory,* or even *My child isn't intelligent.* These worries often stem from deeper influences of negativity. Poor eating habits, frequent illness, or low energy can result from ongoing stress or low self-esteem. Similarly, being overly playful, too distracted, or overly serious can indicate an inner struggle with focus or a tendency toward self-doubt.

Many teens, in turn, become prone to negative thinking, impacting their communication and relationships at home and with friends. When kids begin avoiding discussions with family or frequently fight with siblings and peers, the root issue often traces back to unresolved feelings of negativity or low self-worth.

This negativity may manifest as constant excuses, blaming others, or complaining, a behavior learned over time as a coping mechanism for perceived inadequacies. Academics may hold on to limiting beliefs, like *i am not capable,* which, if unaddressed, can reinforce a cycle of underachievement and lack of confidence. Ultimately, negativity in a child's environment, behaviors, and thoughts deeply impacts their immediate performance and health and their long-term potential, emphasizing the need for positive reinforcement and open communication to break the cycle.

Over time, these influences can shape a teen's outlook, diminishing their confidence and impacting their focus and academic success. By addressing and minimizing the negative influences in their environment, parents can help foster a more positive mindset that allows their children's true capabilities to shine.

This book is designed to tackle the unique challenges teens and parents face today. From mobile addiction to peer pressure and lasting impacts of the pandemic, each issue has a root cause in negativity—and the key to overcoming it lies in ***Imparting positivity consistently.*** With 101 carefully crafted lessons across 14 comprehensive chapters, this book provides clear, practical solutions that guide teens toward building resilience, self-esteem, and healthier relationships.

CHAPTER I

EMOTIONAL RESILIENCE AND MINDSET

The chapter on "Emotional Resilience and Mindset" emphasizes the importance of nurturing children's inner strength, promoting positive outlook, and promoting a growth mindset, focusing on preventing self-pity, setting boundaries, and learning from challenges.

This chapter also addresses setting boundaries ("Are You a Toy?") and responding to "childish" behaviour. A key theme is teaching children to cope with life's inherent unfairness and to adopt a growth mindset where "There is No Failure, Only Feedback", and learning from challenges.

EFFECTIVE COMMUNICATION & DISCIPLINE

- Getting Children To Listen And Concentrate
- Addressing Negative Behaviours (eg: Making Faces)

SELF-ESTEEM & EMOTIONAL INTELLIGENCE

- Avoiding Self-Pity & Modeling Resilience
- Understanding Child Development Stages ('Childish' Behaviour)
- Teaching Children About Life's Inequities

PROMOTING A GROWTH MINDSET

- Reframing Failure As Feedback
- The Passive Behaviour ('Gandhi")

1

HOW DO I GET MY CHILDREN TO LISTEN AND CONCENTRATE?

We conduct training sessions and seminars which allow us to meet thousands of children and parents who belong to various nationalities for the past two decades. Through these interactions I obtained insights by paying attention to their narratives about their challenges. This book represents the wisdom and solutions I have collected during my work while showcasing the most important lessons which both time and experience have demonstrated.

Several parents frequently share these three challenges with me:

- The way I need to deal with my child remains a challenge
- My child refuses to follow what I say, and so I need to learn how to make them listen.
- How do I help my child to concentrate?

Parents should understand that handling their children is not the correct way to view parenting. The main objective of parenting involves developing relationships and providing care. Children possess thinking capabilities and emotions together with personal viewpoints just like adults do. A positive and guiding approach can inspire children to learn.

Children face difficulties when it comes to paying attention. Your children will develop better learning skills and show more interest in schoolwork if you make an effort to build an interesting learning environment. Through my encounters with children I have discovered that teaching them brings significant rewards which many times result in enjoyable moments. Children will listen better when you show enthusiasm during learning activities.

Many people incorrectly believe that teaching children is an extremely challenging task and exists globally. Certain educational facilities create false impressions about learning difficulties. The idea that teaching children is hard is false because the actual reality reveals:

A learning process that combines entertainment and excitement will make children naturally focus on their studies.

Children will develop natural love for listening and concentration when you combine learning activities in an enjoyable manner.

When teaching science to your child you should extend beyond traditional textbook study. Get creative! The topic requires students to perform laboratory tests while viewing educational videos or visiting educational sites connected to the subject. When learning becomes interactive and dynamic you can expect immediate growth in interest levels and student participation.

Children participate in workshops either in confined or extensive meeting spaces. The benefit of individualized attention goes to every child regardless of whether they are in a small or large group. They get direct guidance when learning in smaller groups. Through their teacher's guidance and interactions, with fellow students they learn in larger group settings. Both learning approaches can be effective when used correctly.

The benefits of online learning match those of offline learning because each approach offers its own set of advantages. The traditional offline learning approach combines with online benefits which include uniting students and teachers from worldwide locations and self-directed learning as well as game-based content and continuous assessment and app-based communication.

This book provides the most important educational benefit to parents who read it. My mission is to make you the most capable parent and educator possible so you can give your best to your children. Before moving on to the following chapters take a brief moment to tell yourself:

"I will give my best to my child!"

This book contains information that will assist parents in developing contented independent children. The process of guiding them leads to both satisfaction and personal fulfillment because it goes beyond mere responsibility.

SUMMARY OF CHAPTER 1 / I

Through our training sessions and seminars, I've interacted with thousands of children and parents, gaining valuable insights. This book embodies the wisdom I've gathered, addressing common parental concerns like handling children's behavior and maintaining their focus. Parenting should be nurturing rather than controlling. Making learning engaging enhances children's attention. Creative methods, small or large workshop settings, and both online and offline learning environments can be effective. This book aims to equip you with the tools to raise happy, self-sufficient children.

Secret No. 1

Making the learning process engaging and exciting will further encourage your child to listen and focus.

2

SELF-PITY WILL KILL YOUR CHILDREN'S SELF-ESTEEM

Have you ever found yourself feeling sorry for yourself? Throughout the years I have encountered numerous reasons which people use to explain their self-pity including:

- I lost a parent at a young age.
- My marriage isn't going well.
- People take me for granted.
- I work hard but don't earn enough.
- I don't have real friends.
- I do most of the work at my job.
- My boss treats me poorly.
- I have health issues.
- I'm struggling with my weight.

The experience of self-pity creates a state of powerlessness in people. The feeling of being ignored by others and life becomes overwhelming which leads to depression. Parents unintentionally pass down feelings of self-pity to their children through unconscious actions which create destructive effects. Common reasons parents feel pity for their children include:

- They have to read a lot at a young age.
- Their subjects are too difficult.
- They must work hard to prepare for exams.
- They have little free time.
- They wake up very early.
- They travel far to school.
- They may not be strong enough to participate in sports.
- A parent isn't present.
- They don't have friends to play with.
- Parents can't spend enough time with them.

Parents should understand that their concerns about their child's difficulties should not create a mindset through their words and emotions.

Self-pity weakens the abilities of your children thus making them more susceptible to life's obstacles. Children who develop self-pity become victims instead of leaders when they start to feel sorry for themselves. Victims believe their circumstances are beyond their control and frequently express the thought "What can I do? Nothing! "

SUMMARY OF CHAPTER 2 / I

Self-pity stems from various personal struggles, creating feelings of powerlessness and often leading to depression. Parents may inadvertently instill similar feelings in their children through their concerns, hindering resilience and fostering a victim mentality rather than empowering leadership qualities.

Secret No. 2

Parents, Be mindful of your words. Avoid saying or implying anything that fosters a sense of self-pity in your children. Be careful not to create a victim mentality.

3

ARE YOUR CHILDREN LIKE GANDHI?

In one of the counseling session, a father expressed that his child was just "too nice" and said 'It's so painful for us. Our child is like Gandhi! He doesn't even know how to fight. I want him to pick a fight sometimes, at least, come home with some complaint, and throw tantrums once in a while. In short, I want him to be a normal child! I fear that people will take him for granted in the future, and the world will be hostile and harsh to him". The father perceived the son's tendency to always agree and accommodate without complaint as a weakness.

Despite the father's apprehensions, he shared heartwarming stories of how his son cared for him during an illness, showing deep empathy and understanding. While this behavior demonstrated emotional maturity and care, the father had consistently failed to communicate expectations about assertiveness and standing up for oneself. It became evident that the father's failure to express dissatisfaction and label certain behaviors as unacceptable was inadvertently enabling his son's compliant behavior. For instance, the father said, " Recently, despite our constant protestation, he played cricket in the drawing room and broke a very expensive antique jar at home with the ball. Both my wife and I loved that piece a lot. We were going to scold him, but then, eventually, we didn't. Compared to the worth of our son, that jar is nothing. We can always earn more and buy whatever we want."

Finally, I understood the problem. I told the father, 'Your son isn't a 'Gandhi,' but YOU are!' He was confused and looked at me in confusion. I repeated with emphasis, 'It is YOU!'

'Did you and your wife feel bad when he broke the jar?'

He said, 'Of course. We felt terrible. It was precious to us.' 'But why didn't you tell him that you felt so bad about the loss? Why didn't you scold him for what he did? Where was your assertiveness?' You must learn to express what you feel. Learn to express your feelings if your children's behavior is not up to the mark. As a parent, you must BE ASSERTIVE.

The session uncovered a deeper issue: the father needed to model assertiveness. Just as Mahatma Gandhi was assertive in his quest for independence through peaceful means, Assertiveness doesn't necessarily mean being confrontational but involves expressing one's needs and setting boundaries and values crucial for survival and success in today's world.

SUMMARY OF CHAPTER 3 / I

In a counseling session, a father lamented about his son's excessive niceness, fearing it would lead to being taken for granted. While sharing anecdotes of his son's empathy, the father failed to teach assertiveness. Upon realizing his own passive behavior through the example of an expensive broken jar, the counselor emphasized that the father needed to express his feelings and model assertiveness for his son's development.

Secret No. 3

If you stand up for your rights, then your children will not have to be theoretically taught this quality. Remember parents, the best way to teach, is through example.

4

'MY CHILD MAKES FACES': ARE YOU A TOY?

In one of my sessions, a mother was very worried about her 10-year-old and said, "He does not respect me or his father. But he respects his father only when he's around." After the discussion with the parent, I took her son out with me and asked him different kinds of questions to find out whether he respects others, particularly his parents. It was quite clear that he loved and respected them a lot!

Returning to the mother, I asked, "What makes you think he doesn't respect you?" She insisted there were "millions of reasons." When I gave her a piece of paper and a pen and asked her to make a list, she looked at me and said, *'I can only list seven or eight.'* I said, 'Fine, go ahead.' but, in the end, she could only list three: making faces at her, not washing his hands before meals, and not studying when told.

When I asked why she saw it that way, she responded, "He does it daily." I then asked how she reacted, and she admitted, "I try to keep quiet, but when he keeps doing it, I eventually shout." This pattern had been going on for years.

From her responses, I realized and told her, loud and clear, 'As far as your son's concerned, YOU ARE A TOY.' She was shocked, 'What?" You are a toy. You are a clockwork toy with a key.' She asked me, 'What do you mean?" You seem to behave like a toy. He turns on your key, and you react. He enjoys this. Sometimes, the key is hard to turn on, and he needs to do more to make you react.' I told her, "Break the pattern. When he makes faces, make silly faces back. Change the game." Initially surprised, she agreed to try something new.

A few months later, she returned with a smile and said, "It worked! It was fun, and our relationship improved. Now, he respects me more. I was the one who needed to change."

The key to breaking this dynamic was her decision to stop being the predictable, reactive "toy" her son had been manipulating. By changing her response, she changed the game and their relationship.

A mother concerned about her son's disrespectful behavior. Regardless of her convictions, conversations showed he cared for them. She first provided reasons for her worry but could identify only a limited number. Upon realizing her reactive behavior was a "toy" for her son, she chose to alter her responses. Eventually, she came back joyfully, observing enhanced respect and connection.

SUMMARY OF CHAPTER 4 / I

A worried mother believed her son disrespected her. Discussions revealed the son actually loved and respected his parents. The mother, initially citing many reasons for her concern, could only list a few minor behaviors. I explained her reactive responses made her seem like a "toy" he manipulated. By changing her reactions, their dynamic improved significantly. Months later, she returned happily, reporting increased respect and a stronger relationship.

Secret No. 4

Observe the dynamics between your children and you. Are your reactions always on cue? Do you always react in a manner they have learned to expect? Are you a toy in their hands? Then here's the solution—break the pattern! You will notice a marked improvement in their behavior.

5

` MY CHILD IS CHILDISH'

Do you know what one of the most common complaints I receive from parents is?

'My child is very childish!'

Once, a mother told me about her son. 'He doesn't listen to me at all nowadays. When I call him, he doesn't answer immediately; he won't get up from where he's sitting. There are times when I need to feed him! He won't put on his shoes on his own.' She continued, 'You must talk to him. I want him to be independent and more responsible. He is too childish.'

I told her, 'I'll definitely talk to your son. Where is he?' She said, 'Well, here he is, in my lap.' I was stunned. He was not even more than four years old. Of course, he would be childish! In fact, He was a child for heaven's sake. It may seem really funny in a way! But the expectations some parents hold, really scare me. Remember, your child is a child and will be childish!

If children are not 'childish', they miss out something important in their lives — the joy of being children! Allow them to be playful, to be their age. When they are playful, learning comes naturally and easily. Have you noticed how young children learn from anything and everything.

Accept the fact that your children are going to be childish! Childish behavior doesn't mean they will suffer from a lack of responsibility or display unruly behavior. They are still learning. What you know today is the result of years of training and life experiences. Expecting the same level of understanding and maturity from your children at a young age can lead to disappointment, as they are not equipped to meet such unrealistic expectations.

It's important to embrace and enjoy your children's childish behavior, as these moments will soon become cherished memories. Many parents often express disbelief at how quickly their kids grow, reminiscing that it feels like they were born just yesterday. Rather than regretting missed opportunities, enjoy their early years and take the time to have fun with them now.

SUMMARY OF CHAPTER 5 / I

Parents often complain their children are too childish, expecting independence and responsibility from young kids. A mother described her four-year-old son as unresponsive and dependent. Childhood is a time for playfulness and learning. Accepting childish behavior is essential; it allows kids to grow and creates cherished memories for parents. Enjoy their early years!

Secret No. 5

Don't be anxiety-ridden that your child displays 'childish' behavior – that is only natural. Enjoy these playful days in the morning sun to the fullest, as later days may bring their own worries.

6

LIFE IS UNFAIR

Is life fair or unfair? You know that everyone expects life to be fair. We expect elections to be fair, organizations to be fair, business deals to be fair, bosses to be fair, and teachers to be fair.

What happens in reality? In reality, elections aren't always fair, not just due to illegal activities but sometimes even due to natural events like bad weather.

I recall organizing an awareness talk for over a thousand people, but an unexpected rainstorm meant only two hundred could attend. Isn't that unfair? Consider these scenarios: someone follows every traffic rule yet ends up in an accident, children suffer from terminal illnesses, babies become orphans, natural disasters claim lives, one plane crash takes away hundres of lives and people face disabilities from birth. These incidents highlight one truth: life is inherently unfair.

Parents often struggle to treat each of their children fairly, yet it's a challenging task. It's crucial to accept that life is unfair and teach your children the same. Acceptance makes it easier to deal with unfair situations without feeling victimized. In our camps, I tell the children upfront that things will be unfair, which surprises them. With examples, they begin to understand and accept this reality.

Life demands that we learn to navigate its inherent unfairness and still find success. Encourage your children to accept this notion and prepare themselves for life's inequities. Children often feel that their teachers are unfair, and sometimes parents agree. But can a teacher truly be fair to every student when parents struggle with fairness, even between two children at home? Be ready for this. Exam results and class assessments are common areas where your children might feel unfairly treated. Instead of letting it upset them, prepare them to deal with it.

Help your children learn to face and overcome life's unfairness.

SUMMARY OF CHAPTER 6 / I

Life is inherently unfair, contrary to our expectations. Elections, events, and personal experiences often reflect this reality. Children must learn to accept life's inequities, as parents struggle with fairness. Prepare them to navigate unfair situations, encouraging resilience in the face of life's challenges and disparities.

Secret No. 6

Encourage children to view unfairness as an opportunity for growth and learning.

7

THERE IS NO FAILURE, ONLY FEEDBACK

We often hear and read stories of success and the rewards that success brings. Nobody likes to talk about their failures and bad experiences. Failing is necessarily assumed to be a bad thing. The world is a whole of competition; consequently, there are winners and losers. How do you take it when you lose? Do you give up?

How is a rough, uncut stone made into a diamond? By polishing it really hard. It's the same with all of us. We need to go through rough phases and should have the courage to face failures; only then will we start shining like diamonds. Times of failure are times to learn. Behind every successful person lies some amount of past failure. The only difference between an ordinary person and a very successful person is that the latter takes failure as feedback and learns to move ahead with a different strategy.

I want to share with you the story of Soichiro Honda, the founder of the Honda Car Company, who said, 'What people see of my success is only one percent, but what they don't see is the ninety-nine percent, which are my failures.'

In 1938, Soichiro Honda invested all his savings into a small workshop to develop piston rings to sell to Toyota. To fund this venture, he even sold his wife's jewelry. After completing the piston rings, Toyota rejected them, stating the quality was below their standards. Honda returned to school for two years, enduring ridicule from his classmates. Yet, his perseverance paid off when his redesigned piston rings eventually won Toyota's approval and contract.

A new challenge emerged when the Japanese government, preparing for war, refused to supply him with the concrete needed to build his factory. Did he give up? No. Honda rallied a group of men to make their own concrete and successfully built his factory.

During the war, Honda's factory was burned down twice, leading to significant destruction. Did he give up? No. He and his team restored empty fuel cans discarded by American soldiers and repurposed them as materials for his factory. Then, an earthquake flattened his factory, prompting him to sell it to Toyota. Subsequent ventures in manufacturing didn't succeed.

Faced with a severe petrol shortage in post-war Japan, making it impossible to drive to get food for his family, Honda attached a small engine to his bicycle. This innovation drew interest from many people who wanted one for themselves. Recognizing the demand, he started a factory to build motorcycles.

To raise funds for his motorcycle factory, he wrote to eighteen thousand bicycle owners. When the bikes were manufactured, only a handful of people bought them, as they were too big!

Finally, he developed the Honda Cub, and the rest, of course, is history. Although Honda experienced many failures, he only took them as feedback and never let go of his dream.

As parents, we often unwittingly pass on the message to our children that it is 'bad' to go wrong to fail. Teachers punish students, directly or indirectly, for making mistakes. Their peers never let them live it down. Friends and loved ones discourage them from venturing into the unknown, all for fear of making mistakes and failing. In the final analysis, we have become people who think we are 'Better safe than sorry' or people who are 'Once bitten, twice shy.'

" Stop-look-listen-learn."

Failures are feedbacks. Through it, we can learn what doesn't work, which makes it easier to discover what does. It makes us stop, look, and listen. If we add "learn" to this sequence, failure becomes the first step to success. Stop-look-listen-learn; that's the way to leverage failure.

SUMMARY OF CHAPTER 7 / I

Success stories often overshadow failures, which are seldom discussed. Failure is viewed negatively, but it can lead to growth, much like a rough stone becomes a polished diamond. Soichiro Honda's journey illustrates this: after facing repeated rejections and setbacks including losing his factory, he persevered by innovating and learning from failures. His achievements stem from treating obstacles as feedback. Society teaches children that failure is bad, discouraging risk-taking. However, embracing failure as a learning tool can pave the way to success. Remember, "Stop-look-listen-learn" to turn failures into valuable lessons.

Secret No. 7

Whenever children fail to reach their target, you must teach them to take the results as feedback and not give up. Once they understand that failure is something they can learn from, they will stop making the same mistakes in the future and never be depressed by the burden of taking failure too seriously!

CHAPTER II

BUILDING SELF-ESTEEM AND CONFIDENCE

"Building Self-Esteem and Confidence" emphasizes the importance of empowering children to develop a strong sense of self-worth and belief in their abilities. It highlights the role of adults, environment, and experiences in shaping children's self-worth, promoting happiness, resilience, and success.

BUILDING CHILDREN'S SELF-ESTEEM

- Identify and Address Underlying issues
- Positive Reinforcement & Encouragement

PARENTAL SELF- REFLECTION

- Differentiate Behavior From Child's Worth
- Acknowledge & Address Personal Fears
- Avoid Transmitting Anxiety

POSITIVE MINDSET AND RESILIENCE

- Celebrate Achievements (Big & Small)
- Foster a Growth Mindset
- Instill Perseverance & Resilience
- Inspiring Stories & Role Models

8

HOW TO BUILD YOUR CHILDREN'S SELF-ESTEEM

This chapter is your chance to determine how dedicated you are as a parent! Now that you understand what self-esteem is, it's time to put that knowledge into action and help your children shine in whatever path they choose.

Commit to taking the following steps right now!

1. ***Engage Your Partner:*** Share this knowledge with your spouse! Put this book down, feel the excitement, and talk to them in person or call them immediately. Both of you must be fully invested in giving your children the best support possible.
2. ***List Your Children's Achievements:*** Write down twelve accomplishments for each of your children from the moment they were born. Here's a space to fill in:

(I would suggest both parents do this exercise separately, and then you can share what you have written).

Sl. No.	*Child 1*	*Child 2*	*Child 3*
1			
2			
3			
4			
5			
6			
7			
8			
9			
10			
11			
12			

1. Once you've completed this exercise, reflect on whether it was easy or challenging to come up with twelve achievements. Now, did you have to struggle to think of twelve answers, or was it easy for you? If you previously weren't aware of why your children weren't reaching their full potential, I'm sure you have the answer now.
2. Remember, similar thoughts about their worth might be running through your children's minds. Consider what you've done to show them they are loved, valuable, and capable.

3. Discuss Achievements with Your Children: Have you ever talked with your children about their accomplishments? ***If not, now is the perfect time to start!*** Share your thoughts on why you believe they are capable and what informs your belief in their potential. Make this a habit! Regularly highlight their achievements and express how proud you feel.

In the future, your children may come home saying things like, "My teacher said I wouldn't succeed," or "A classmate made fun of me." How will you react? Instead of trying to intervene with the teacher or classmates, focus on building your children's self-esteem at the root. By actively nurturing their confidence, you'll empower them to handle criticism more effectively.

SUMMARY OF CHAPTER 8 / II

List twelve achievements for each child and reflect on the ease of this task. Discuss these accomplishments regularly with your children, reinforcing their value and potential to build resilience against negativity from others.

Secret No. 8

Think about the achievements your children have made, and if you haven't shown appreciation yet, take a moment to do so. This simple acknowledgment will have a powerful effect on their self-esteem!

9

DO YOU DISLIKE YOUR CHILDREN OR THEIR BEHAVIOUR?

What is the difference between the following two statements? `You are stupid!' `When you know you have an exam but don't prepare for it, that is stupidity!' When you tell your children 'You are stupid', you are in a way, defining them. When children hear that from the parents, they subconsciously start accepting the statement as a fact. When they do something and it goes wrong, they think that it's because they are stupid and stupid people make mistakes! It happens when they make an error in their schoolwork, when they play a game, when they draw, when they dance.

Whenever they make a mistake, it confirms their notion that they are stupid! But what is of concern is the fact that when your children assume they are stupid, they can't do anything about it. Another example of this idea is when you tell your children, 'You are slow.' This statement slows down your children for a lifetime. When they are young, they believe that their parents know absolutely everything. Whatever their parents say is true. When you tell them, `You are slow', it becomes one hundred percent true for your children. They accept this as a fact. They invariably up to start seeing this as a fact.

The key difference between the two statements at the beginning of this chapter is that in the first statement you say that the child is stupid, while in the second you say that their action is stupid. There is a huge difference between these statements. Once you learn this, it becomes easy for you to pull your children away from all kinds of non-productive behaviour. They also gain the powerful insight that it isn't them, but a particular trait, action or habit, that their parents don't like.

As a parent, when you scold your children about something, learn to direct your reprimand against the action or behavioural trait that you don't like, and don't accuse your children instead.

SUMMARY OF CHAPTER 9 / II

Labeling children negatively can instill a fixed identity, while addressing behaviors encourages growth, helping them understand their actions rather than internalizing harmful beliefs.

Secret No. 9

As a parent, when you need to correct your children, focus on addressing the specific action or behavior you want to change rather than blaming the child personally.

10

ARE YOU TRANSMITTING YOUR OWN FEARS TO YOUR CHILDREN?

During one of our camps, we were doing a simple mathematical exercise as part of a study-skills activity. I noticed one child who wasn't participating. He was just watching others. As I was curious, I approached him and saw that he looked worried. I asked him why he wasn't joining in, and he replied, "I don't know how to do this."

I assured him, "It's easy, I'll explain it to you," and sat down to help. But as I went over the math, his expression didn't change. He still looked troubled and wasn't really listening. I asked him what was bothering him. His response surprised me: "I don't think I'll ever understand this."

I asked why he felt that way, and he gave me an interesting answer: "I'm bad at maths, just like my father." Then he added, "Maths isn't in our genes!" I was shocked. I sat with him and talked to understand where this strong belief came from. He explained that when he would show his father his low math scores, his father would say, "It's okay. Don't worry, I was bad at maths too, and your mother doesn't understand basic calculations. Maths isn't in our family or our genes."

Can you see how powerful these words were for this little boy? At such a young age, his father unknowingly planted the idea that he would always struggle with math. But is this really true? Not at all. In fact, numerous studies on children show that there is no scientific basis for such claims.

Parents, be mindful of the messages you pass on to your children. Don't burden them with psychological inheritances that can hold them back. Aaron Stern, in his book *The Making of a Genius*, shares the benefits of early learning by telling the story of how he raised his daughter Edith Stern. Aaron Stern was a Polish Jew who escaped the Nazis and settled in the United States, where he raised two children, Edith and David. In his book, he describes how he educated Edith from a young age with the hope that she would become a genius. He used what he called the "Total Educational Submersion Method," spending a lot of time talking with her, reading to her, encouraging her to ask questions, and exposing her to a variety of experiences.

Here are some milestones in Edith's education:

- At ten weeks old, he began showing her meaningful toys and picture books.
- By eighteen months, he introduced her to flash cards and taught her how to use them.
- At twenty-two months, she started reading.

- By the age of three, she had read the entire *Encyclopedia Britannica* from A to Z.
- At eight years old, she entered the fourth grade.
- By eleven, she was in junior high school.
- At sixteen, she earned a BA degree with a focus on mathematics and went on to become a math instructor at Michigan State University. In just two years, she completed a Master's degree in theoretical mathematics and fulfilled the requirements for a Doctor of Philosophy.

This story is remarkable not just because of Edith's accomplishments but because of the way her father chose to raise her. Despite the trauma he experienced during the Holocaust, Aaron Stern didn't let that pain shape his children's future. Instead, he immersed them in a world of learning, exploration, and possibilities.

SUMMARY OF CHAPTER 10 / II

During a camp's mathematical exercise, a child expressed worry and said, "I don't think I'll ever understand this," citing his father's similar struggles with math. His father's comments instilled a belief that math struggles run in their family. This highlights the importance of the messages parents convey to their children. In contrast, Aaron Stern, despite his traumatic past, raised his daughter Edith to succeed in academics, employing his "Total Educational Submersion Method," which led to her remarkable academic achievements, including advanced degrees in mathematics.

Secret No. 10

Parents, it's crucial not to pass your own sense of inadequacy or the pains of your past onto your children. Instead, encourage them to live in a world filled with curiosity, ideas, colors, music, and learning.

11

CELEBRATE LIFE!

Celebrate life! `What for?', is a common response I get from people, when I tell them this. My question is 'Why not?' People have always agreed with me when I have said 'Be happy in life', but are confused when I say `Celebrate Life!' When and why must you celebrate? Whenever you feel fortunate deep inside, fortunate to be whatever you are, celebrate.

Let me ask you a question that might change your outlook: How many things are actually going well in your life? Even when people tell me, "Nothing is working," I ask them to consider if their body is functioning well. For instance, if your eyes are working, do you feel fortunate compared to someone with visual challenges? This realization can transform your life perspective. Feeling fortunate reminds us to make life meaningful, appreciating all that is working well.

How can you bring a celebratory spirit into your life?

- Focus on Positivity: Concentrate on what is going well rather than what isn't. Gradually work on improving the rest.
- Create Magical Moments: Bring joy by creating wonderful experiences for yourself and others. I cherish the gifts and

letters I receive and have started personally responding to each one, creating more joy for both myself and others.

- Embrace Opportunities: Celebrating life makes you eager to seize opportunities, creating a positive cycle of joy instead of falling into negativity.

SUMMARY OF CHAPTER 11 / II

Celebrate life by recognizing your fortunate aspects, focusing on positivity, creating joyful experiences, and embracing opportunities. This transformative perspective fosters happiness and meaningful connections, turning challenges into celebrations of existence and gratitude.

Secret No. 11

You don't need a special reason to celebrate, being alive right now is enough. Once you learn to cherish life, you pass this greatest gift onto your children, teaching them to celebrate and live better.

12

IT IS POSSIBLE FOR ME!

Every child has an immense potential. Then why is it that some children do exceptionally well and others don't? Say, for example, a child goes out to play a game and loses. And let's assume that this happens a few times. By listening to what people say, the child slowly starts developing the notion that he cannot play that game well at all. This may lead the child to give up for good or even start accepting himself as mediocre! Can the parents do anything to help?

This is the time for the parents to act, and help the child develop the right mindset, If so many others could keep their dreams alive in spite of to many obstacles, to can I?

Let me take this opportunity to share the story of Roger Bannister with you:

'People always believed that it was not humanly possible for an individual to run one mile under four minutes. Researchers and doctors also supported this notion, saying that it is impossible to accomplish this, as the human body mould not be able to deal with it and it may even lead to instant death.

Roger Bannister, a medical student, was not ready to accept this theory. In the year 1954, after extensively training his mind, Roger Bannister completed to one-mile distance in 3 minutes and 59.4 seconds. From then on, it was known as the 'Miracle Mile'. He accomplished this only through his belief of possibility and training.

The most interesting fact is that within a year of Roger Bannister accomplishing this, over three hundred people were able to run one mile in less than four minutes and some of then were even able to break Roger's record! The truth is, till the time Roger Bannister proved to the world it was possible, everyone believed that it was humanly impossible. Once he was able to prove it, people started believing that if it's possible for Roger Bannister, possible for me!

As a parent, you should impress the belief in your children that anything is possible if you put your mind to it. Once children start believing this fact, it will open up a new vista of possibilities for them.

- Is it possible to go to another planet in a few seconds?
- Is it possible to travel and make a holiday home on Mars?
- Is it possible for a student who consistently fails to get distinction in all subjects?
- Anything is possible if you have the right strategy

Not too long ago people believed that it was only birds who could fly, as their body is designed in such a manner. There were, however two bicycle mechanics who thought differently. Both of them had a strong conviction that they could invent a machine that would make humans fly like birds. The basis of their belief was that: Anything is possible, it is a question of the right strategy. Wilbur and Orville Wright flew their first aircraft at Kitty Hawk, North Carolina on 17th December 1903.

When they accomplished this great teak, people were astonished. Did this happen by chance? No! If it was not for their sheer hard work and commitment, who knows we would still be taking weeks and months to travel from one continent to another. Imagine, how slow life would have been! Imagine our life without travelling by air! What do you think made the difference?

If children start developing the belief that anything is possible at a young age and that it's just a question of having the right strategy, think about the changes in the children's mindsets. Children's minds are very inquisitive. They want to find out all the details about everything they come across. This is the time of life when questions keep appearing in their minds. Next time your children ask you whether it is possible for them to get the first place in class, or even to build a castle on the moon you know the answer, don't you? Just help them get the right strategy.

SUMMARY OF CHAPTER 12 / II

Every child has immense potential, but external perceptions can hinder their confidence if they encounter failure. Parents can help building a growth mindset, encouraging children to believe in their limitless possibilities. The story of Roger Bannister illustrates how belief and determination led to the first sub-four-minute mile, inspiring many others. Similarly, the Wright brothers demonstrated that with the right strategy, flying was achievable.

Instilling this mindset in children can transform their outlook and unlock their true potential.

Secret No. 12

Inculcate in your children the belief that nothing is impossible and that everything can be achieved if they believe in their dreams. Having the right strategy and a strong belief will help your children turn what they thought was impossible into possible!

13

NEVER, NEVER GIVE UP

These are indeed great words from Winston Churchill: 'Neve, never, never give up!'

One thing common among people who are very successful in life is that they are never ready to give up. This attitude helped them achieve all that they had and fulfilled many of their dreams.

When business is going great, when times are excellent, does anybody give up? No! So, when do people give up? When businesses close down, When everything seems to be going wrong, When life becomes tough, When challenges become more than what you think you can handle!Giving up leads to failure! If you want your children to be successful. teach them the phrase, 'Never, never give up.' Teach them to say this to themselves when they feel like giving up when they think that problems are too big and not easily manageable!

How can you teach them this? Not by simply saying these words to them. You need to teach them through your actions. If you want them to believe it, practice it in your own life. For instance, 'Giving hope is a behavioral pattern which children learn easily from their parents! I have worked on this problem with several families in the past.

In one of my recent experiences, a mother was complaining to me about her daughter,"My daughter isn't serious about anything she does! She joined a music class and quit halfway through. She loved drawing, constantly asking us to buy her materials. She started with great enthusiasm, but after just a few weeks, she lost interest and now she can't even find her art supplies! She lacks focus and gives up too easily."

I spoke with her daughter to understand better. She explained, "I do what I'm interested in. Once drawing becomes boring, I stop doing it." She reaches a certain level of skill, and when it starts to get more challenging, she finds it tough and chooses the easier route by giving up. This pattern meant she never developed expertise in any of her activities, like music, swimming, dance, basketball, or drawing classes she joined only to leave later on.

I later discovered this pattern also applied to her mother, who had changed jobs about four times in the past few years. Her reasons varied, claiming the boss was unfair, the company wasn't great, or the job was too stressful or didn't pay enough. I helped her realize that these were just excuses and emphasized that if she wanted her daughter to change for the better, she needed to take charge of her own life.

SUMMARY OF CHAPTER 13 / II

Winston Churchill's words, "Never, never, never give up," highlight the mindset common among successful individuals.

People typically give up when facing challenges, leading to failure. Teaching perseverance to children requires demonstrating it through actions, as parents influence behavior. A mother's complaint about her daughter's lack of focus revealed a similar pattern in her own life, showing the need for change in family attitudes towards persistence and commitment.

Secret No. 13

This is a one-liner. **NEVER GIVE UP**

14

WHAT STORIES WILL INSPIRE YOUR CHILDREN?

Once you've decided to share inspirational stories with your children. Decide who you're going to talk about. I share a lot of inspirational stories with children. When you share someone's life, it's important to help your children get the right message. Choose a character with whom your children can relate. There are certain events in a person's life which are particularly illuminating. You must know which ones to highlight. I tell the children stories of young achievers and other interesting people who they may look up to. Let me share a few pointers with you, which you can, in turn, follow up on.

Sachin Tendulkar: At the age of five Sachin decided to play cricket. He lived with his aunt and uncle while he was young so that he could attend coaching classes. And then comes the tale of his meteoric rise from the tender age of sixteen. Children find his story very inspirational.

Bill Gates: At the age of thirteen he decided what he wanted in life and started doing what he enjoyed the most – creating software. His being so rich today was possible through his dedication, hard work and high sense of focus. And while many children know that he is one of the richest men in the world, it is important to also tell them about the Bill and Melinda Gates Foundation, which has made a difference to so many lives by promoting healthcare initiatives worldwide.

Steven Spielberg: At the age of twelve, he set a goal for himself – to be a director and impact the world through his movies. Follow up the story from here. Show your children a film like Spielberg's E.T. and Jurassic Park which will work on their imagination.

Tiger Woods: At the age of eight he decided to be a world-class golfer. His story inspires many people. Make him your household name. Tiger Woods keeps himself at number one not by sheer luck, but by practicing golf for over sixteen hours a day! Now that kind of commitment is incredible.

Wilma Glodean Rudolph: A premature baby, Wilma was born in a poor family in Tennessee. When she was four, she had double pneumonia and scarlet fever, which left her partially paralysed with a motionless left leg. When she was nine, however, she set herself a goal to be the greatest women's runner in the world! Her mother used to always encourage her and told her not to fret because her brightness made up for her disability, and she would fulfil her dream. Wilma made it to the 1960 Rome Olympic Games. She won both 100 and 200 meters and became the World's greatest women runner of that time! She also won her third gold in that very Olympics and became the first American woman to win three gold medals in one Olympics!

SUMMARY OF CHAPTER 14 / II

To share inspirational stories with children, choose relatable characters and highlight significant life events. Examples include Sachin Tendulkar, who pursued cricket from age five; Bill Gates, who dedicated himself to software creation at thirteen; Steven Spielberg, who aimed to direct at twelve; Tiger Woods, who committed to golf at eight; and Wilma Rudolph, who overcame adversity to become an Olympic champion. These narratives teach resilience and determination, motivating young minds.

Secret No. 14

Make role models a part of your child's world by connecting their stories to everyday life.

CHAPTER III

GOAL SETTING AND ACHIEVEMENT

"Goal Setting and Achievement" focuses on helping children see their own success, set meaningful goals, and build the practical and emotional skills they need to reach them. This chapter boosts self-esteem and confidence by introducing structured ways to turn dreams into real accomplishments and encouraging a lasting sense of control.

This chapter highlights goal setting as an essential life skill that promotes independence, motivation, and the ability to overcome challenges. By guiding children to discover their passions, set clear and realistic goals, and celebrate their achievements, parents and educators can prepare them for success in all areas of life.

INSPIRATIONAL STORYTELLING

- Share Real- Life Stories Of Inspiration
- Your Teen Can Be Successful Anywhere

POSITIVE COMMUNICATION

- Speaking Positively About Children
- Changes Happens In A Heartbeat!
- Why Should I Study?

COMPETITIVE MINDSET

- Play to Win
- Proactive Approach
- Take Charge

15

THEY CAN BE SUCCESSFUL ANYWHERE

A wonderful fact that I've discovered about human life is that a person can be successful in any profession. What it takes is to love what you do and to put the very best into it. Can a professional cook be extraordinary? On the contrary, can a doctor be an average achiever? Of course. A chef can become a significant role model and a prominent person through his great love and commitment to what he is doing!

Why am I saying this? It's because children are often forced to choose a specific path for their career because of societal and parental pressures. I have come across several children who want to be designers or journalists, but their parents insist upon their becoming doctors, to be successful in life. My question to these children is, 'What would you love to be? A doctor or a designer?' If the children strongly feel that they should become designers, then undoubtedly that's where the children would be successful. If forced into the medical profession, it is more likely that they would turn out to be mediocre doctors!

The reality is that a top-class hair stylist reaches greater heights of creative satisfaction than a mediocre cardiologist, who enters the operating theatre to perform a lifesaving operation though his heart is not in it. What exactly does this mean? Your children's successes aren't just related to the type of professions they engage in but what they make out of it!

This has been the state of my own life. I was playing a pivotal role in a prominent software company based in Singapore. I was doing well enough; I was 'successful,' but in a worldly sense, I knew that I wasn't at my best. I realized that my passion was guiding people in certain areas, and to be at my best, I needed to choose to be a mentor to people. I had to help people take charge of their lives.

I made a massive shift in my career. I chose to be a mentor, and I know that I am at my best in this field. I am geared up to achieve more and more in my life. I am happier being a coach to young minds and the CEO of my own company than being the head of the business division of a world-class MNC.

Give this powerful choice to your children. Allow them to choose a career they love, which will make them successful! Guide them to make an informed choice.

A person's success in any profession stems from their passion and dedication. Children should not be forced into careers like medicine if they aspire to be designers or journalists, as true success arises from love for one's work. A fulfilled life means guiding children to follow their true interests instead of societal expectations. My own career shift from corporate to coaching exemplifies the joy and success found in pursuing one's passion. Empower your children to choose their paths!

SUMMARY OF CHAPTER 15 / III

Success in any profession arises from passion and dedication. Children should be encouraged to follow their true interests, rather than be pressured into careers like medicine when they aspire to be designers or journalists. Personal fulfillment is derived from doing what one loves. My own shift from a corporate role to mentoring exemplifies the joy that comes from pursuing one's passion. It's crucial to empower children to make informed career choices aligned with their passions for a successful future.

Secret No. 15

Let your children live their dreams and follow the paths of choice. They will undoubtedly be much happier that way and reach great heights of creative and professional satisfaction.

16

INSPIRE YOUR CHILDREN WITH REAL-LIFE STORIES OF INSPIRATION

As a parent, do you tell your children stories? I am quite sure you will say 'Definitely, when my little ones were young, I used to tell them stories every night.

Did you tell them the stories of the Fox and Grapes, "The Lion King, The Dog and the Bone? I am sure you would have told them. If not these, but other stories in the same vein.

But have you ever told your little ones the stories of Honda, Indira Gandhi, Narayanamoorthy, Abraham Lincoln, Martin Luther King Jr., Wilma Rudolph or Colonel Sanders? How about being parents who also inspire their children through the careful selection of stories?

I'm sure you watch a lot of films at home or in the cinema hall. Have you ever watched inspirational stories with your children? Are they interested in watching such videos? It is up to you to create that interest in them No doubt, deep in your heart you desire that your children lead successful lives, better than the one you or your parents lived. To do that they need to know about visionary people who succeeded in fulfilling their dreams.

I feel that what shaped my life wasn't so much the science or maths that I learnt in school and college, but the inspiring life histories of people that I read and heard about. Thus, in our training programmes 1 shares stories about the lives of some amazing individuals, with the children. Every visionary has a powerful message for the youth. Why don't you share these with your children? They'll find, in the treasure trove of inspirational stories, clues to lead them on in their search. If you want to give your children an extraordinary passion for life and dreams, inspire them.

SUMMARY OF CHAPTER 16 / III

Parents often share fictional stories with their children, but real-life tales of figures like Soichiro Honda and Martin Luther King Jr. can inspire and open possibilities. Introducing these stories fosters curiosity, purpose, and drives children to pursue their dreams passionately.

Secret No. 16

Among the many stories that you tell your children, remember to particularly include some inspirational ones

17

CHANGES HAPPEN IN A HEARTBEAT!

A common mindset among parents is that negative changes in their children happen instantly, while positive changes take a long time. Parents often share stories of immediate negative shifts.

"I can't believe this! Until yesterday, he was so nice. I don't know what has happened. I have never seen him act in such an arrogant manner with us. 'My child has started smoking. His whole life will go to waste if he continues."

If you see your children with people you perceive to be a bad influence, you instantly decide that their life is doomed, and yours along with it. I've found that parents often accept the fact that negative changes occur in an 'instant.'

On the other hand, they believe that positive changes take years to come about. However, I've also encountered another scenario: parents being amazed by the swift positive transformations in their children after attending MiTran Global Imparting

Positivity Camp programs. "I can't believe how quickly my child has improved! Is this change real? Will it last?"

I urge parents to understand that positive changes can happen in a heartbeat just as quickly as negative ones. Believe in these positive shifts, encourage them, and treat your child as if this newfound behavior is their new norm. You'll often see these changes endure and multiply over time.

Accept positive change.

Positive changes happen in a moment, too!

SUMMARY OF CHAPTER 17/ III

Parents often believe negative changes in children occur instantly, while positive ones take time. However, positive transformations can also happen rapidly, as seen in our engagement like 'Positivity Hub . Embrace and encourage these changes.

Secret No. 17

Demolish the myth that positive changes invariably take a lifetime to come about! If your children suddenly exhibit a positive trait, do not assume that it is temporary. Make a note of it, encourage them and wait for the result. The change will be here to stay!

18

WHAT SHOULD YOU SAY ABOUT YOUR CHILDREN TO OTHERS?

What you say about your children to others greatly impacts who they become. They start to exhibit the traits you attribute to them. Your perception and description of them holds significant power and shapes their actions and self-image. Let me share an experience with you:

A set of twins participated in one of our program. Their father, a businessman from UAE, expressed frustration over their stubbornness. "They do what they want. Last year, they insisted on going to Australia, and we had to went to the trip! It's been like this since they were little. If one doesn't want to go to school, they just don't go! Managing this attitude is very challenging!" he said.

As we discussed, I got to understand how this behavior developed. When I asked if the twins used to share things when they were very young, the parents strongly said no and mentioned the same to their teacher. Initially, the teacher observed no significant issues, remarking, "They're quite cooperative in class." But after hearing from the parents, she later remarked, "They wouldn't share the crayons in class. They are indeed stubborn."

This made me realize that the sad reality is the children's behavior hadn't actually changed; only the perception had. Before the parents' comments, the teacher saw normal child behavior. However, once influenced by the parents' opinion, she started attributing any action to their 'stubbornness.' In a way, the parents and teachers created this identity. The children fit into this narrative laid out by their parents and began to act accordingly.

SUMMARY OF CHAPTER 18/ III

What you convey about your children shapes their identity. The father's frustration over his twins' perceived stubbornness influenced their teachers' views, leading to a narrative that defined their behavior, illustrating how perceptions can create identities in children.

Secret No. 18

Be mindful of what you discuss about your children with others. You create a lens through which they are viewed. If you paint their behavior in one color, others will see only that hue. Avoid confining your children to a narrow identity; let them thrive in a full spectrum.

19

WHY SHOULD I STUDY?

Do you know what one of the most common questions that runs in the minds of all children is?

"Why should I study?" is a common question among children, often stemming from a lack of understanding about the purpose of their education. With a clear answer, studying can feel worthwhile and exciting. Assume that you're a working professional, Your boss announces that there is an important exam coming up in which you must do well. But your goal results won't translate into a promotion or a pay increase. How will you feel? Will you feel all excited about preparing for the exam? Or will you question the very pointlessness of the endeavor? I am sure that until you get to know the Purpose, you will never feel excited enough to prepare well. The same is true for your children. Just as how we adults require motivation/purpose to succeed at work, children need to comprehend the importance of their studies beyond mere grades. It won't be an exciting enterprise without understanding the strong purpose behind studying. And if their studies aren't exciting, your children will associate them with a sense of boredom.

As a parent, it's your responsibility to make your children that studying is a means to achieve meaningful goals in life. Education opens doors to opportunities and greater success. A common experience for many children is their parents' promise of a reward for studying or doing well in exams: 'If you get more than 90%, I will get you a computer.' 'If you study well, I will take you on a holiday.' What does this mean to the child? It suggests to them that by studying, they are doing their parents a favor. Avoid using rewards like money or gifts as motivation, as this can lead children to feel they're studying for their parents' sake rather than their own. Instead, surprise them occasionally with small gifts that foster a love for learning.

Engaging your children in conversations about the motivations behind studying can make them more receptive to the idea. Help them see the bigger picture; they will likely find studying more exciting and purposeful.

SUMMARY OF CHAPTER 19/ III

Children often question the purpose of studying, mirroring adult feelings about work-related tasks without clear benefits. It's essential for parents to convey that education leads to meaningful opportunities, rather than merely rewarding grades with gifts. Engaging children in discussions about the value of studying fosters motivation and makes learning more exciting and purposeful.

Secret No. 19

Patiently discuss the purposes and motivations of studying with your children. Share the larger picture with them, and you'll find them more receptive than you imagined.

20

PLAY TO WIN

What is the difference between one who wins and one who doesn't? Are their skills and capabilities that different?

The truth is that the difference is in the mindset - a winner plays to win, whereas the one who doesn't has played not to lose.

What is the difference in the time taken by an Olympic gold medal winner, and the person who wins silver? It is almost nil, only a fraction of a second. Do they prepare differently to win different medals? Do they go through different kinds of training programmes to sharpen their athletic skills? Are the efforts involved different? No. They train for the same number of hours and use the same world class training methods.

Similarly, consider the person who came fourth, who didn't get anything and went back unnoticed by the world. What's the difference between the person who came fourth, and the gold medalist? Again. it's a matter of only few seconds, sometimes only a fraction of a second. Does that mean that the person who won the gold won only on the basis of luck? No.

The difference lies in their mindsets.

The champion Play to win. I will win come what may. It is a 'do or die' situation.

The one who came close, but didn't make it I will not lose come what may. I shouldn't lose. I have to stay there and see it through.

Are these differences big enough to produce results that are tremendously different? The 'play to win' mindset triggers different thoughts and different sets of actions, compared to the 'play not to lose' mindset.

Your actions you take depend on your mindset. This small difference in a person's mindset can cause a huge difference in the final results. This is also true for children. I have seen children setting their examination goals at say, 90% in maths, or 98% in maths. I always ask them if there's it difference in the number of hours they put in as compared to their classmate who decides to score 100. No!What makes the difference? The mind!

Teach your children to have the mindset of a GOLD medalist!

From what I see, when students set a goal to achieve 97%, that's also, though not apparent, but a goal to lose 3%! In a manner of speaking, it's a goal to commit silly mistakes. Before they even begin to write the exam, they've set a goal to lose a few marks. That can create a whole lot of difference in their results and their achievement levels. It's the same difference between receiving the gold medal and the fourth place!

SUMMARY OF CHAPTER 20/ III

The difference between winners and losers primarily lies in their mindsets. Winners adopt a "play to win" attitude, while losers focus on not losing. Even Olympic medalists often have negligible time differences, yet their mental approaches yield vastly different outcomes. This principle applies to children as well; those aiming for 100% set a higher standard compared to those who accept a lower goal, ultimately influencing their results and achievements.

Secret No. 20

Create in your children a mindset of 'playing to win .'Make them realise he difference. It isn't only about skills or aluck;it is about the mindset,The winning mindset!

21

TAKE CHARGE!

How do you talk to your children? Words have tremendous power over the mind. Negative words and questions can hurt or disturb children, while positive words can have a great impact on them. Positive words create enthusiasm, boost self-esteem, and push children towards more significant achievements.

What you say to your children matters, as does what you say to yourself.

Say, for example, your teenager is answering back. The natural tendency of a parent to ask questions to themselves are :

'Why does my child always answer back!'

'Why does he never listen to me?'

'Why is she acting so insensitively?'

You will get answers to these questions, but they are not helpful. Once you get started on a negative thinking pattern, you will get stuck on them. Instead of these questions, start practicing alternative questions:

'Isn't it great that my child dares to express his feelings?'

'In what way can I understand my child better?'

Questions like these will change the way you feel about the situation and help you come up with solutions. Positive words create enthusiasm. By boosting your children's self-esteem, you will push them towards greater achievements.

For example, after a long day at work, you might come back home and say to yourself, 'I'm totally exhausted.' These words will intensify your feelings of tiredness, and you will end up being more exhausted than ever before.

So, instead, use less intensive words or words with a positive meaning that can help you focus on the positive side of the issue. For example, instead of saying, 'I am exhausted,' say, 'I'll feel better,' or 'If I rest for a while, I can finish my work.' This will help you deal with the situation much better.

A powerful phrase I am going to share with you is **Take Charge.**

When you say bye to your children, do you say 'Take Care'? Stop! Never say 'Take Care' again! When you say' Take care, ' it presupposes that your children must be cared for! This makes your children feel less in control of things. In a way, one might say 'Take Care' conveys self-pity.

Instead, say TAKE CHARGE! Experience the difference. The most mind-blowing experience will be that once you start saying this to your children, your children will also respond in the same positive way. You will also hear 'Take charge' from your children when you say goodbye. It gives you lots of power and puts you back in control.

Some positive words you must use are:

- Instead of 'I will try to do it,' say, ' I will do it. . . .' (Stop using the word try)
- Replace 'I have a problem at the office' with 'I have a Challenge' (Stop using the word Problem)
- Never say, 'I hate to work'. Instead, say, '1 love any work'.
- Never say, 'I don't know'. Instead, say, 'I am yet to learn.'

SUMMARY OF CHAPTER 21/ III

Talking positively to children significantly impacts their minds, boosting self-esteem and motivation. Instead of asking negative questions about their behavior, parents should reframe them positively to foster understanding. Similarly, adults should avoid negative self-talk that amplifies exhaustion, opting for affirming phrases like "I'll feel better." Change your farewell from "Take Care" to "Take Charge" to empower children. Replace negative terms with positive language, e.g., "I will do it" instead of "I will try" to promote a constructive mindset.

Secret No. 21

This one's the simplest and the easiest; I want you to remember it always. **TAKE CHARGE!**

CHAPTER IV

UNDERSTANDING AND MANAGING EMOTIONS

Parents and educators can better assist children in navigating their emotional world by Understanding and Managing Emotions of teens . It promotes effective emotional control and self-awareness. This chapter combines communication insights, practical tactics, and neuroscience.

The chapter highlights the fact that emotional intelligence is a skill that can be developed, modeled, and taught. Adults can help children develop the resilience and self-awareness necessary to flourish in a difficult world by comprehending the causes of emotions and behaviors, emphasizing connection, and employing both rational and creative approaches.

PREPARING CHILDREN FOR CHALLENGES

- Facing the Negativity
- Parental Priorities (Defining Priorities)

PERSONAL GROWTH

- For Things to Change I MUST Change First
- Behind Every Behavior There is a Positive Intention

UNDERSTANDING CHILD'S WORLD

- Decoding the Left Brain
- Decoding the Right Brain
- Meaning of Communication = Response Received

22

YOUR CHILDREN MUST LEARN TO FACE THE NEGATIVE WORLD

What is self-esteem? It's how your children feel about themselves.

Do your children feel lovable? Do they feel confident and capable? Are these factors really important?

Only when your children feel loved, confident and capable can they be achievers. How can you make your children feel this way? Remind your children of their achievements and make them feel special.

I have often come across parents who say, 'My child hasn't achieved anything important enough to feel great about. 'Other parents complain that nothing their child did was particularly remarkable! Now that is not the right attitude. Your children needn't be the architect of some of the world's most important achievements for you to applaud them. Their achievements may be small, but the way you look at them is what eventually makes them feel good about themselves. For example, a prize in a drawing competition, skill in cycling, commitment to reaching school on time, an appreciation card from the teacher or the ability to play a musical instrument - all of these are worthy of your appreciation.

Why is self-esteem so important?

Remember, your children live in a negative world. Very often they have to face negative comments, cruel teasing from classmates, and insensitive words from teachers, neighbours or relatives. Can you stop this? There may be times in the past when you might have. But can you do it forever? No. Your children must learn how to ignore such needless comments and handle unpleasant situations.

There have been times in our training programmes when children have fought amongst themselves and complained to coaches: 'so-and So said that I'm like a horse (whatever that means)… she said I am very dark… he never spoke with me.' – the list goes on and on. As you would understand, this is one of the toughest parts of conducting training programmes for children. But as a parent, what can you do to deal best with such a situation?

I have seen parents feeling bad when something like this happens. They sometimes come and tell us that we shouldn't let it happen in the programme. There have been times when parents have met the parents of the children who have been 'troubling' theirs, in an attempt to help their child. But is that the solution? Can you stop this sort of behaviour, when the stage is the whole adult world, and not a small classroom? The solution lies elsewhere.

When children feel loved and confident they're largely unaffected by hurtful comments or teasing. They hold their heads high as they know who they are. Nothing external can bother them. There is no other solution to this problem, as you can't always be there to protect your children, and so your children must know how to face these problems on their own.

Now, think how differently you must handle the situation when your children face teasing words or insults from anybody. High self-esteem is a MUST for your children to help them face the world when it is negative towards them.

SUMMARY OF CHAPTER 22/ IV

Children face negativity through harsh comments and teasing, making resilience and self-esteem vital. Self-esteem influences how they perceive their worth. Parents can nurture it by celebrating achievements, big or small. While negativity is unavoidable, reinforcing their strengths at home equips them to handle outside challenges, fostering confidence to face a complex world. High self-esteem is essential.

Secret No. 22

Consciously cultivate a strong sense of self-worth in your children. It's essential to equip them to face the harsh criticisms and negativity that life may throw their way.

23

ONCE YOU ARE A PARENT, LEARN HOW TO DEFINE YOUR PRIORITIES

One of the most common challenges parents face is the constant push and pull between work and home. I am sure you will agree that your priorities were different before your children were born. What were your priorities then?

Career?

Achievement?

Wealth?

Health?

Social commitments?

After your children were born, do you feel that you are not able to do justice to your work? Do you feel that you need to compromise on certain areas of achievement? Are you emotionally torn between the need to do more as a parent and achieve more as an individual? Once you become a parent, you will have a huge need to consciously rework your priorities in life. If you refrain from doing this, you will continue to be emotionally torn all the time.

Have you ever faced the choice between meeting an important client or going home early for your child's birthday? Or deciding between a business trip and being home when your child has a big exam or competition? These moments require tough decisions. You may skip the business meeting but feel uneasy at home or take the trip and regret missing a special day with your child.

Why are these emotions so powerful? It's because they reflect what you value in life.

Once you become a parent, you need to rethink your priorities. I met a successful saleswoman during a project who was a single mother. She worked hard for her daughter's well-being. "I aim to give my daughters the best education, which requires my best performance at work. I often sacrifice time with them due to my job's demands, but I'm not unhappy about it. I do this for them, so choosing between home and work is not difficult for me. My priority is work because it's for my family," she explained.

On another occasion, I talked with a banker, a father of two, who declined promotions and a chance to open a new branch abroad. When asked if he regretted these decisions, he said, "I could have achieved more career-wise, but it would mean being away from my family for years. Nothing is more important than my family and being there to guide my children. We must share special occasions together—without that, life feels empty." He had no regrets.

Both parents deeply care for their children but prioritize differently. So, when will you define your own priorities? What holds more importance for you? Career or family?

You must set your priorities so that you aren't torn apart emotionally. You might insist both are important, but if you must choose one, which will it be? Once clear, these decisions become easier as you progress through life. Defining priorities helps you reach your goals.

- What do your children mean to you? What do you want to provide for them the most?
- Ensure their financial security and educational opportunities while allowing them to pursue their dreams, even if not immediately lucrative.
- Be present for all their special moments.
- Always be with them, guiding them daily.
- Teach them to be autonomous and learn, regardless of your presence.
- Any other definition?

SUMMARY OF CHAPTER 23/ IV

Parents often struggle with balancing work and home life after having children, leading to a re-evaluation of priorities. Initially focused on career and wealth, many now confront tough choices between professional commitments and family milestones. The emotions tied to these decisions reflect deep personal values. Parents like a single mother and a bank father emphasize that their choices, whether sacrificing time for work or declining promotions, center on family. Defining clear priorities is crucial to avoid emotional turmoil and achieve life goals.

Secret No. 23

Once you become a parent, clearly define your priorities. This will help you confidently make difficult choices without emotional stress every day.

24

FOR THINGS TO CHANGE, I MUST CHANGE FIRST!

I have had occasion to ask many children: 'Why did you score such low marks in your exam?' I received various answers, such as:

- The subjects are very dry and boring.
- The question paper was tough
- .Our teacher did not teach us properly.
- They made me sit in the wrong place during the exam.
- They never give much time for preparation.
- During the holidays, my parents had taken me away.
- Guests had come to visit just when I had my exams.

Many parents tend to back their children when they blame teachers or the school for their problems, saying things like, "The teachers don't teach well" or "The syllabus is too hard." I often ask both parents and children if they can change their school or teacher. Parents usually respond that it's difficult, while children, not knowing the reality, enthusiastically say, "Yes, I'll just switch schools!"

In conversations, I point out, "Can you really change your teacher or school? And if you did, what ensures the problem won't recur? How many times can you keep changing?" This often leads them to realize that the real issue lies within themselves, not external factors.

I then challenge them: "In your school, with the same teachers, are other students doing well? Why can't you?" This drives home the point that real change begins from within. The key lesson is, "If something needs to change, I must change first."

This concept applies to family, too. Children might feel nagged by their parents or annoyed by siblings. Instead of wishing others would change, I ask, "Is there a way you can change how you react or deal with these situations?" This mindset opens them up to numerous possibilities for change.

Parents, too, should adopt this mantra: "For things to change, I must change first." If you want your children to behave differently, perhaps the change should start with you. Reflect on your actions and consider if they might be driving your child's behavior.

Instead of waiting for external change, take personal responsibility. Change yourself for the better, and your children will likely follow your example.

SUMMARY OF CHAPTER 24/ IV

Children often cite various reasons for low exam scores, blaming teachers, subjects, or other external factors. However, it's crucial to realize the issue lies within themselves. Emphasizing the need for personal change, I encourage both parents and children to reflect on their actions and reactions, fostering an understanding that meaningful change starts from within.

Secret No. 24

Never wait for the world around you to change for you. It simply means continuing in a situation over which both you and your children have no control and wearing a girdle of victimhood. Come forward and take responsibility for what happens. Change yourself for the better. Take control of your life.

25

DECODING THE LEFT BRAIN: UNDERSTANDING YOUR CHILD'S WORLD

There are two parts in the human brain, The left brain and The right brain; these two parts control two different sets of functions. The left brain controls functions that include logic, maths, linearity, language, sequencing, and analysis. The right brain controls creativity, rhythm, holism, imagination, and colors.

Which part of the brain do you think children primarily engage when learning school subjects? Most traditional study methods in schools require the use of the left brain. Research indicates that children rely on their left brain about 90% of the time. Children can generally be categorized as either left-brain or right-brain dominant, meaning left-brain or right-brain functions influence them more. But Does this result in different behaviors?

Let's consider some behavior patterns associated with left-brain children: What does a left-brained child's study area look like? It is typically neat and organized, with everything in its designated place. These children prefer to keep their surroundings tidy. For example, if you touch their desk, they may quickly ask why you're disturbing their setup! If someone borrows an item and fails to return it, they become upset. A left-brain dominant child arranges their books according to a timetable and is prepared to attend school early. They like being on time and usually enjoy school because traditional teaching methods suit them. They often excel academically, being average, above average, or high achievers.

Now, I am sure you'll be wondering if your child is a left-brainer. If not, ask yourself, "Is my child a left-brainer?"

Now that you know the characteristics of a left-brain child, What challenges do these children face? Left-brain dominant children often tend to be shy. This trait doesn't cause much trouble in the early years, but as they grow, they seek social acceptance and worry about others' perceptions and treatment. They analyze social interactions deeply and may withdraw if they feel misunderstood. Parents often comment, "When visitors come, my child stays in their room and struggles to engage with new people." Does having this behavior mean they have many friends? Not really; their friend circle is small, and they are not very expressive even with these friends. Many struggle with public speaking at school. Now, Identify how such behaviors can be changed.

SUMMARY OF CHAPTER 25/ IV

The human brain consists of the left and right hemispheres, each controlling different functions. Left-brain children, who dominate in logic and organization, prefer orderly environments and adhere to schedules. However, they often face challenges like shyness and social anxiety, leading to limited friendships. Addressing these behaviors can help foster better social interactions and confidence in public speaking.

Secret No. 25

Are you concerned about why your organized and logical child may struggle with social interactions or group activities? Explore whether your child is left-brain dominant.

26

DECODING THE RIGHT BRAIN: UNDERSTANDING YOUR CHILD'S WORLD

The previous chapter explored the characteristics of left-brain dominant children; now, let's dwell on the behavior patterns of right-brained children. Now, You might wonder if these kids would be quite the opposite of left-brained ones, right??

How do you imagine their study space appears? Yes, you guessed it- a chaotic, cluttered mess. If you ask them to find their science book, it might take ages; when they do, the book's condition might shock you. The book that was once shiny and new could now look quite worn and have pages missing.

These children often lack organization. For instance, if they have a class test on Monday, they might inform you about a missing notebook the night before. You can imagine the stress this causes for parents! In the morning, just as they need to leave the house, they search for books and pencils. Parents often struggle to get them out of the house prepared. Though they leave home looking neat, how do they return after school? With messy hair, untucked shirts, dusty shoes, and socks, and whatnot!

A mother shared this experience: One day, her child returned from school missing a sock. When she asked where it went, he quickly replied, "It's in the lunchbox." Right-brained children are very intelligent but often dislike school because traditional teaching methods don't capture their interest. Their attention span might be short, and they often daydream in class. Easily distracted, they might disrupt others by throwing paper balls or pencils. Teachers find it challenging to manage them. These children might not always excel in school, finding some subjects difficult. However, they're talented in sports, music, and any activity that ignites their creativity. If a project needs volunteers, they're the first to step up and will do whatever it takes to complete it. They are usually outgoing, make friends easily, and socialize well. While you might read on a journey, your child will chat with other passengers, often leaving with a special goodbye from everyone.

Right-brained children find conventional schooling methods dull and challenging. Can they focus effectively? In the following pages, we will delve into this topic further.

SUMMARY OF CHAPTER 26/ IV

Right-brained children exhibit chaotic organization, often struggling to find materials like books and notebooks, leading to stress for parents. While intelligent and talented in creative activities, they may dislike conventional teaching methods, resulting in short attention spans and daydreaming. Their outgoing nature helps them socialize easily, despite academic challenges.

Secret No. 26

Are you concerned about why your bright and creative child dislikes the traditional school routine? Discover if your child is right-brained dominant.

27

BEHIND EVERY BEHAVIOR, THERE IS A POSITIVE INTENTION

My theory is that every kind of behavior you, I, and others engage in has a positive intention behind it, although the behaviour itself may not be positive. Incredible as it may sound, even destructive or criminal behaviour has a kind of positive intention behind it. Once you believe that there is a positive intention, you're forced to think from a different perspective and work accordingly. If your children are engaged in a certain activity which you don't approve of, try to understand the positive intention behind it.

The children will have an excuse for everything they do the action might be hurting someone, stealing money, telling a lie, bullying others in class or showing certain 'abnormal' behavioral patterns. But you must understand that in their scheme of things, there is a positive intention that drives their behaviour. If you notice that your children are engaged in some kind of a negative activity, don't panic. The worst thing you can do is to punish the children immediately. Once you do that, the children are going to shut their doors against you.

They will never open up, and irrespective of the severity of their punishment, their behaviour may worsen to the point where you may end up in a vicious cycle; not knowing how to get out of it. Instead, cool down. Sit down and think about the situation. Put yourself in your children's shoes and work out why they are behaving like this. Before you can discover what is driving your children, you must first believe that there is a positive intention behind that The first step is to develop a rapport with your children. Your children must see you as a friend, not as an enemy always ready to attack. You need to be patient and understanding. Then you can start asking certain questions to find out what it is that your children wants to achieve through their behaviour. And once you understand it, you can guide and help your children to change their behaviour in a way that satisfies the positive intention.

Let me give an example here. Say, for example, you went out shopping. When you came back, you noticed that your elder child has hurt the younger one and the little one is crying in pain. On one hand, you know that there is a reason behind everything we do, and on the other hand, you're furious with your elder one for the act, whatever be the impulse behind it! What could be the reason behind such atrocious behaviour from a child who is usually very good? Is the child feeling insecure and threatened by the sibling? If he or she is feeling insecure, what could have induced this feeling? Is it the way that you are behaving? Have you been unintentionally paying less attention to the elder one because you've been preoccupied with the younger one? Have you started comparing both children in front of others? When is the last time you hugged your child?

Ask yourself questions that will help you find out the real intention behind the child's behaviour. Once you understand this, consciously modify your behaviour; make your child understand that he is very precious to you. Do this consistently and the negative behaviour will automatically disappear. Say, for example, your child had stolen money from home and had gone out for a movie with friends. As he comes back if you start yelling at him, it will get you nowhere. Sit and talk to your child. Start by saying things like, 'I know that you are not this kind of a person, so, what made you take money from home?' It is because his peer group makes him feel like a loser, or do his friends make fun of him for not going along with them for outings? Or is it because he feels that he needs to have more control on his life? In other words, whenever there is negative behaviour it means that there is a need deeper in the children which they are not able to communicate.

If we can look for the real purpose behind the behaviour, we can find other more constructive solutions towards meeting that need. Always look for the positive intention behind the children's behaviour. I have worked with children who are labelled criminals by society. If I need to bring about positive changes in their minds, the only way to reach them is through their hearts. It is essential to understand why they did what they did. Was there a positive intention behind it? I once worked with a child who murdered his own uncle, to save his mother. Was there a positive intention?

Was saving his mother at the cost of murder, a positive intention? There were no easy answers to these questions.

I hope you do understand that I'm not condoning the act. But if we wanted to help the child to change, we needed to understand why he did what he did. He was in a juvenile welfare institution and the job of the institution was to bring him back to the mainstream and make him a dutiful citizen. In order to bring in a positive mindset, understanding the positive intention behind an abhorrent act is very important.

Do not judge too soon. Try to analyse the motivation behind your children's actions, and in them you will surely find the answer to their behavioural problems.

SUMMARY OF CHAPTER 27/ IV

Every behavior stems from a positive intention, even negative actions. Instead of punishing children for undesirable activities, try understanding their motivations. Building rapport and listening carefully can help identify underlying needs, such as insecurity or the desire for attention, leading to healthier behaviors and improved relationships. This approach applies across various contexts, including troubled youth.

Secret No. 27

Refrain from judging too soon. Try to analyze the motivation behind your children's actions, and in them, you will surely find the answer to their behavioral problems.

28

THE MEANING OF COMMUNICATION IS THE RESPONSE YOU GET

Communication is based on the responses we get from the other person. Although we may have intended something specific by our words, we can't guarantee that the other person will understand us in the way we meant it. You can probably think of times when you have misunderstood the meaning behind someone's words.

For example, we might intend to compliment someone, but if they take it the wrong way, what can we do about it? Can we argue with the person concerned? A better approach would be to compliment them in a different way.

In the same way, if you don't like the response you receive from your children, then you must be willing to change your method of communication until you get what you want.

Let me give you an example of a conversation between a mother and a daughter.

Susan: 'I can't do my homework. I've left my books behind in school.'

Mom: 'You've become very forgetful, Susan. I wish you were more organized.'

Susan: 'I know. I'm worried about not finishing my work now, and look at Jason. He's mocking me.'

Mom: 'Leave him alone. He isn't the one who left his books behind at school. I wish you were as organized as him .'

Susan: 'Why don't you leave me alone? Why do you always compare me with that brat?'

The conversation can go on and on with no real purpose. Be flexible when talking to your children so that they understand your message.

Here's another example.

A mother and a daughter are discussing a party.

Mom: 'Reena, I'd like you to come home from the party at 8 pm tomorrow.'

Reena: 'Mom, there's no way I can do that. The party goes on until 10 pm, and I must be there until the end.'

Mom: 'It sounds like being there until the end is really important.'

Reena: 'Yeah. All my friends will be there! Mom, you just have to let me stay until ten. Soon, we will be going to different schools. This may be one of the last times we can hang out like this!'

Mom: 'I get that this party means a lot to you, and I'm concerned about your safety. Let's get more details about this party - and your ride there and back - and see if we can work out something together.'

Reena: 'OK Mom. I'll talk to my friend and check whether we can come back together somewhat earlier.'

Mom: 'That sounds good.'

The conclusions are for you to draw. Which parent is more effective?

SUMMARY OF CHAPTER 28/ IV

Communication relies on responses; intentions may not align with perceptions. Misunderstandings can arise, underscoring the need for flexibility in dialogue, especially with children. Effective communication adapts based on feedback. In examples, one mother uses comparisons leading to conflict, while another engages collaboratively, prioritizing understanding and safety. The latter approach fosters better communication, exemplifying effective parenting.

Secret No. 28

Think about how you can be flexible enough with your children during conversations so that they understand the message you want to convey. The response you receive from your children will tell you whether you are communicating in the right way!

CHAPTER V

EFFECTIVE COMMUNICATION AND LISTENING

"Effective Communication and Listening," explores how parents can enhance a stronger, trusting relationships with their children through intentional, empathetic, and skillful communication. This chapter emphasizes that communication is more than just words it's about modeling, listening, and creating an environment where children feel valued and understood.

Effective communication is the foundation of a strong parent-child relationship. By listening actively, responding with empathy, modeling positive behaviors, and embracing confusion as part of growth, parents can nurture confident, articulate, and emotionally intelligent children

EFFECTIVE COMMUNICATION

- The Best Parents Are Like Giraffes!
- What You Do Matters a Lot More Than What You Say!

PARENTAL SUPPORT AND GUIDANCE

- Encouraging Growth: The Parent as a Supportive Coach
- No Child is Unable to Learn

PRACTICAL PARENTING STRATEGIES

- The Regimen at Home
- Balancing Parenting: How Do I Learn This Art?
- Good , I Am Getting Confused

29

THE BEST PARENTS ARE LIKE GIRAFFES!

I watched a short film about giraffes on one of the popular channels. The film taught me a valuable lesson. Let me share it with you.

A giraffe had just delivered a little one. It looked so cute, fragile and soft! Any animal lover would have ached to hold and cuddle the tiny creature

After a while, its little legs began to gain strength, and it tried as hard as it could, to get up. It was quite a struggle, before it could fully stand, it fell several times.

Finally, after all this effort, the little one almost succeeded in standing up. To my shock, its mother, who had been watching closely all this time, immediately gave it a hard kick! The baby tumbled down. Then started to try again.

This went on for a long time, and through the commentary, I gradually got to understand what was happening. Without the kicks from the mother, the little one would have managed to stand easily. But in a time of need when it would have to face an attack from other animals, it wouldn't have developed the strength to escape. Its mother wanted to toughen it so that it would be able to fight back. She knew that the only way her little one would have got stronger and learnt how to survive was through the hard way!

Unfortunately, what I've seen between parents and children has been precisely the opposite. Thinking that they're helping the children, many parents do the children's work on their behalf. In the long run, they end up making the children mentally and physically dependent on them. Now and then children need that kick to emerge stronger! And that's why I say, 'The best parents are like giraffes!'

Parents, particularly from Dubai, Sharjah and Abu Dhabi often tell me, 'We are deeply concerned about our Children's future, as they have been highly protected! Children here never struggle for anything, and life is so easy for them. During our days it was different.'

This is a legitimate fear.

Do remember as a parent, you can't always be there to make things easier for your children. By protecting and making their lives smoother, you take away your children's ability to face tough situations in life. You weaken the survival instinct! So, sometimes don't hesitate to be like the mother giraffe.

SUMMARY OF CHAPTER 29/ V

A short film about a mother giraffe teaches parenting lessons: allowing children to struggle fosters independence. Overprotective parenting can hinder resilience, as kids need challenges to develop survival skills. Embrace tough love for healthier growth.

Secret No. 29

Sometimes, if you see your children struggling with something, don't jump to do the task for them. Be by them, give them courage, and learn to let them experience odds, too. Let your children grow up to be tough people. As Robert Schuller says – 'tough times don't last, but tough people do!'

30

ENCOURAGING GROWTH: THE PARENT AS A SUPPORTIVE COACH

You're not just a parent to your children, you're also the **COACH**!

What do I mean by a coach?

One of the most inspiring movies I have ever seen is *Rocky*. Rocky's coach never hesitated to be tough when he needed to be so. He pushed Rocky, sometimes in a seemingly negative way, only to bring out the best in him.

A good parent is like a COACH.

Unfortunately, many people think that to be good parents they must support their children by making their tasks easier for them. This is not a wise strategy. An effective parent is not one who passively 'supports' the children thus, but one who guides them in the right direction and allows them to fight for themselves. Just as a coach, while deeply involved with a sportsman's career, uses a careful combination of rigorous practice and developing mental toughness, to create a winner!

Here's a story I particularly like.

A teacher wanted to demonstrate to her class how a pupa comes out of its case. Its case, which was about to break, was kept on the table and the teacher got all the students to stand around. They saw a small crack in the case and were cheering aloud. The teacher knew that it would take about half an hour for the insect to emerge, and told the students, 'Nobody must touch it. I'll be back in half an hour. Watch what happens carefully, and note down what you've learnt.' The children agreed and the teacher left.

After half an hour, the teacher came back and was shocked because the insect lay dead on the table and all the students looked guilty. The teacher was upset and asked the students 'What happened?'

After a while, one student came forward to say, 'Teacher, I'm sorry. I'm responsible. You told us clearly that we mustn't touch and should only observe. But it was tough to watch. The little insect was struggling to come out of its case. It was so difficult for it, that I was scared it would die and so I pulled out the insect from its case. After a few seconds, it was dead. I'm not sure what I did was right. Sorry!'

The teacher told the students, 'What killed the insect was the concern you showed to it. It only gains the strength to survive by struggling. There is a reason and purpose for its struggles. You must allow the insect to fight, to enable it to survive.

I share this story with lots of parents. Parenting is the same. If you always pull your children out of tough situations, your children will never develop the emotional muscles to fight back. Your children will never get an opportunity to prove themselves. They may even start giving up easily.

SUMMARY OF CHAPTER 30/ V

Being a parent means acting as a coach, guiding children to face challenges independently. Support should involve fostering resilience, not just easing difficulties. Like the teacher's story about the pupa, intervening too much can hinder development; struggles are essential for growth and emotional strength.

Secret No. 30

Be a coach to your children. This means staying engaged and supportive, while also allowing them to fight their own battles. Help them develop their skills and teach them to stand strong on their own.

31

THE REGIMEN AT HOME

I once met a father, a businessman, who was extremely upset with his only daughter. We had a chat, during which he shared a lot of information with me about his fifteen-year-old girl. He said that she was good at her studies and understood her responsibilities. But then he added, 'Everything is fine, but I know she will fail terribly in life." I was shocked. I asked him, 'WHY? What makes you say this?'

'She is very bad at time management. You may have all the skills you need, but if you are bad at time management, you will fail in life. Do you see the sun? Every day, it rises at a particular time and sets at a particular time. (Really?) Everything in this world is time-bound. Take the case of my daughter. When taking an exam, she invariably leaves a few questions due to a lack of time. She never eats, sleeps, or wakes up on time.'

As he was talking, I began to understand his model of the world. The one thing that made him successful in life was doing everything on time.

I wanted to understand him better, so I asked him to elaborate further.

He responded, 'I have learnt one thing in my life, and it is that which has made me a successful businessman. Time is God. I have to pay salaries on time. I must deliver goods on time, or I'll be out of business.'

I asked him, 'Have you done anything yourself to help her to improve her time management skills?

'A lot. I have attended several training programs on time management. I have a lot of tools that help me plan my time. I have taught her all of these.'

What he said next may sound incredible, but it's the truth. I have even prepared her a chart that shows what she should do and what time. My chart includes the time she needs to get up, what time she needs to go for a bath, the times she is allowed to watch TV, and what time she has to go to sleep. She has hardly ever followed it. Nowadays, I stand right behind her to ensure she does things according to the timetable. I want her to be successful.'

I wanted to shout out aloud, 'That's crazy!' but of course, I couldn't.

Instead, I agreed with him. Time is money, health, wealth, everything. But what will make your daughter successful is learning how to manage time rather than being managed by time.'

If you run your life according to the clock, there will be no variety in it. Everything in life will be certain and predictable. Every day will be the same. There is no way that any child's creativity will be enriched in such a disciplined life. She will feel bored with everything. It's time for you to help her!'

As a parent, you should know that while managing time is important, there must be flexibility and variety to make life joyful. Manage time, don't be managed by time. Help your children learn the same.

SUMMARY OF CHAPTER 31/ V

A father expressed concern over his daughter's future due to her poor time management, despite her academic abilities. He emphasized the importance of punctuality in his successful business life, illustrating how he has implemented strict schedules for her daily activities. While acknowledging the significance of time management, I suggested that rigid adherence to schedules stifles creativity and joy. I argued that it's essential for children to learn to manage time flexibly rather than being controlled by it, to foster a fulfilling life.

Secret No. 31

If you always run your life according to the clock, there will be no variety, spontaneity, or excitement, and creativity will not flourish. Teach your children to manage time, but don't let them be managed by time.

32

BALANCING PARENTING: HOW DO I MASTER THIS ART?

Mother: You are watching TV for the past one hour. Better switch it off and do your homework. *Father:* Why are you troubling him so much? Let him watch for some more time.

The child thinks: My mother is always nagging me. Father understands me so much better!

It is not only while watching TV but this happens for every activity the children do.

- Till what time should they sleep in the mornings?
- What kind of food should they eat?
- What kind of TV programme can they watch?
- When and for how long should they play?
- When and for how long should they study?

It is very natural that both parents have different thoughts about what is right and what is wrong. It is totally based on your personal experience, how your parents have defined these to you. Sleeping during the day may be 'wrong' according to the mother. The father feels however, on a holiday, why shouldn't the children sleep during the day? Now, if both parents give different signals, the children feel totally confused! Whoever makes the more 'favourable' choice, becomes closer to the children, the favourite, and more importantly, the other parent becomes the 'villain'.

Define the family rules to children very clearly, and both parents have to follow them as well. Children must understand, that be it the father or the mother, the answer is going to be the same. They should not get into the mindset that 'If father does not allow me to go for a movie along with my friends, I will get the permission from mother!' This, in the long term, spoils the relationship not only between the children and the disciplined parent, but also brings in lots of misunderstandings between the parents too.

How do you go about this elaborate process of framing family rules? - To a great extent, define the broader rules together. If you are putting up a curfew time for returning home, definitely consult your spouse. - If the permission to go for a party or a movie is denied by one of the parents, and the other feels that the children can go, do consult each other before coming to a final decision.

The children must understand that even if one parent feels it is not right to do so, they cannot do it. - Never depict the other parent as a villain : rude, harsh or angry always. 'If you are not doing your homework, I may not be bothered, but let your father come. . . .' This makes your children think that the other parent is an arrogant, angry person. You have to learn to convey to your children that you too are not happy with that behaviour. Speak for yourself. - Convey in every possible way to your children that when it comes to discipline issues you are both united, and you are very clear regarding the kind of behaviour you expect from your children. - When you present a gift, ensure that your children gets the message that it is from both parents together. - Ensure that your children gets some personal time with both of you, individually. Psychiatrists always say that children feel comfortable sharing certain things with the father and certain other things with the mother.

In the long run what does this balanced art of parenting create? Respect in the children for both parents. Acceptance of family rules by all members. A deep bond with both parents, individually.

SUMMARY OF CHAPTER 32/ V

Mother and father often have conflicting views on parenting, causing confusion for children. Kids might favor the more lenient parent. To avoid favoritism, parents should establish consistent rules together, present a united front in discipline, and ensure children know both parents support decisions, fostering respect and stronger family bonds.

Secret No. 32

Both parents need to work together to establish family rules and stick to them consistently. This ensures fairness for the children and avoids any favoritism.

33

WHAT YOU DO MATTERS A LOT MORE THAN WHAT YOU SAY!

One fact that I have become aware of about people in general, is that they always, knowingly or unknowingly, follow the adage, "Are we practising what we are preaching?' For a company focusing on imparting positivity, who helps people take charge of their lives, I find that every day people appraise us critically. The media checks whether we are doing what we say. If we don't practise what we preach, there is no way our programmes would have been as successful as they are now. Parents always want to know how disciplined and motivated we are, so that we can impart our knowledge and skills to their children.

Even during the children's programmes, I find that we may share several inspirational stories with them, but what has the maximum impact when we share about our own journey.

The story of my life being an underachiever, someone with low self-esteem who eventually became a successful entrepreneur and a mentor, works very well. People know I can help them achieve the same kind of transformation in their lives. Thus, parents and children often trust our organization to help them. We break limiting beliefs every day. We continue to cultivate useful habits daily. We set a new standard in the world of imparting positivity, year after year, both with regards to children and adults. They don't follow what you say, as much as what you do.

- If you want your children to be more enthusiastic about going to school, learn to go to work enthusiastically.
- If you want your children to eat healthy food, eat healthy food yourself.
- If you want your children to spend less time watching TV, or more time watching useful and informative programmes, do the same yourself.
- If you don't want them to quarrel with others, stop being engaged in arguments yourself.

Thieves' children won't see stealing as a mistake. Murderers' children don't see murder as a crime. Similarly, the children of timid parents experience feeling shy and lacking confidence as a way of life! Why am I telling you this? Let me describe some of my own experiences.

There was a mother who complained that her son drank almost two cans of coke every day! 'I just want him to stop it. I'm ok with fruit juice.' I asked her how the boy had access to those cans. Does he go to the shop and buy them himself? `No, we always have at least two crates in our fridge, to offer visitors!'

I've frequently heard from fathers say, 'I want my children to be more confident. If you make my children get up on stage and speak a few lines, I know that they will do wonders in life.' During that time, the mother wouldn't even look at me in the eye. I asked the mother, 'Can you do that?' Do you know the answer? 'No way!' She said, immediately. I understood why the child was like that.

As parents, you should make a special effort to create a new identity for yourselves by casting off your limiting beliefs. This way you can become a powerful role model for your children, who will emulate what you do.

SUMMARY OF CHAPTER 33/ V

People assess my effectiveness as a teacher based on my own actions. As a former underachiever turned mentor, I emphasize that practicing what I preach fosters trust.Children learn more from observing adults. For positive behavior, adults must model the habits they want their children to adopt.

Secret No. 33

Live the life you hope your children will learn from. They will follow your example over your advice.

34

GOOD, I AM GETTING CONFUSED

How do you feel when your children are learning a lesson and look confused or tell you that they are getting confused about something? Does it bother you a lot? Do you start worrying about why your children are getting confused? Stop right there and stop worrying. Start feeling happy the next time your children look confused. Because it simply means your children are learning something new. You must be wondering why I say this. If you ask your child who is in fifth standard what 1+ 1 is, will your child be confused? Or will your child be confused if you ask them to do the simple multiplication of 2 x 3? So, When does confusion arise?? When you ask the same child a complicated new sum, at least initially, the child will get confused.

When children do exercises from the previous year's textbook, will they get confused then? No! This indicates that only when children have to do something new, based on a new concept that's been recently taught, or do sums that they have not practiced before do they get confused. Many think being confused about something or not understanding it entirely is bad. Confusion often arises when learning something new or tackling unfamiliar tasks, and it signals that the brain is stretching beyond its current capabilities, stimulating thought and growth.

Even as adults, we get confused, whether it's filing tax returns or learning to drive. For instance, when we started to file tax returns, how many times did we get confused? Starting from how to fill out the form and what and what not to include. And when we began to learn how to drive, weren't we confused? We didn't know how to operate the brake, clutch, accelerator or the steering wheel. During that learning period, how did we feel? It felt complicated and confusing, Right? Yes. But do we get confused while driving now? I'm sure we don't anymore. Initially, these tasks seem complex and contradictory, leading us to postpone them or feel overwhelmed. However, confusion is simply part of the learning process. It pushes us to stretch our brains beyond their current limits, helping us master new skills over time, and this applies to our children, too. Children often avoid difficult chapters because they associate confusion with negativity, but this hinders their growth.

And also parents should understand that,Those who excel academically aren't free from confusion; they embrace it as an opportunity for learning. They tackle challenging topics head-on, seeking help and persisting until they understand. By doing so, they stimulate their brains and become smarter. Embracing confusion as a natural and beneficial part of learning can transform it from an obstacle into a tool for growth and mastery.

Every child can learn with the right strategies. Helen Keller, blind and deaf from 19 months, struggled until teacher Anne Sullivan employed patience and flexibility. By age ten, she mastered Braille and graduated at twenty-four, advocating for the blind and deaf, showcasing the impact of adaptable teaching.

SUMMARY OF CHAPTER 34/ V

When children show confusion while learning, it reflects their engagement with new concepts, indicating growth rather than a setback. This confusion arises when facing unfamiliar tasks, similar to adults learning new skills. It's crucial for parents to recognize that confusion is a natural part of the learning process, encouraging children to embrace challenges rather than avoid them. Those who excel learn to see confusion as an opportunity, fostering persistence and intelligence.

Secret No. 34

Instead of feeling anxious, get excited about confusion. When confused, it means that your child is learning something new.

35

NO CHILD IS UNABLE TO LEARN

Every child in this world has the capacity to learn. If a child isn't able to learn, this only means that the child lacks the right strategies. There were times, in our programmes, when we used to puzzle the whole audience, by having one hundred children learn a long list of words in the same sequence, in a few minutes. In a group of one hundred children I know, many of them were branded as being unable to learn.

There are people who have in the past helped certain children affected by physical problems to learn. Let me share a deeply inspiring real-life story:

Helen Keller was born in June 1880. When she was nineteen months old, severe illness left her blind and deaf She was is very unruly child and her parents found it very difficult to control her, until Helen met her teacher Anne Sullivan when she was six years old. And her teacher created a miracle.

Initially them was a lot of resistance from Helen when it came to learning, but later, because of the dedication, patience and his of her teacher, she took the first tentative steps.

Here are some of her achievements:

By age ten, Helen Keller had mastered Braille, the alphabet, and learned to use a typewriter. By twenty-four, she graduated, with her teacher Anne Sullivan supporting her by interpreting lectures and discussions. Helen later dedicated her life to improving conditions for blind and deaf people, lecturing in over twenty-five countries. Her success was largely due to Sullivan's flexible and adaptable teaching approach. Anne Sullivan is rightfully remembered as a miracle worker.

Now, How come a child with so many disabilities was able to learn? It was due, to her teacher's flexibility and willingness to modify her attitude, until she got her student to learn.

SUMMARY OF CHAPTER 35/ V

Every child can learn with the right strategies. Helen Keller, blind and deaf from 19 months, struggled until teacher Anne Sullivan employed patience and flexibility. By age ten, she mastered Braille and graduated at twenty-four, advocating for the blind and deaf, showcasing the impact of adaptable teaching.

Secret No. 35

Next time you say to yourself, 'My child can't learn,' give it some serious thought. Remind yourself of Anne Sullivan, Helen Keller's teacher. Never forget that every child has the capacity to learn.

CHAPTER VI

MENTAL AND PHYSICAL WELL-BEING

"Mental and Physical Well-being," emphasizes the importance of nurturing both the mind and body to support children's overall development. This chapter integrates practical strategies for parents to have a balanced, healthy lifestyle and emotional stability in their children.

A holistic approach to well-being balancing physical health, emotional support, and positive family interactions equips children. By modeling healthy habits, maintaining open communication, and celebrating both big and small moments, parents lay the foundation for lifelong mental and physical wellness.

PARENTING & CHILD HEALTH

- When Your Children are Ill
- Break the Pattern: Freak Out With Your Children - Once in a While
- When Are You Going to Visit an Orphanage?

MENTAL WELL-BEING STRATEGIES

- The Seven-Day Mental Uplift
- No Blame, No Excuses, No Complaints

PHYSICAL WELL-BEING INDICATORS

- Excessive Sleeping: Not a Disease but a Symptom
- Time to Say "I LOVE YOU"

36

WHEN YOUR CHILDREN ARE ILL

I'm sure that when your children are ill, you've spent time next to your child's bed overnight, or maybe even for several consecutive days. This can be one of the toughest things that any parent experiences, and is something that most will do their level best to avoid.

Think of a time when your children were suffering or experiencing pain due to ill health. I'm sure that you thought, given the choice, you would like to bear the pain yourself rather than see your little one suffer! How do you express your feelings during these times? Do you let your children carry on with activities, which may be physically possible but tough? Or do you do everything for them? Ask yourself honestly - do you show a disproportionate amount of concern? And if you do, realise what you're doing. You are, inadvertently, extending the period of ill health. I'm sure this is a harsh fact for you to accept!

Do you think that I'm blaming you too much? Unpleasant it may be, but it is a fact. Let me tell you why. When your children are ill and behave badly, what do you do? For example, they might be fighting with a younger sibling, watching TV for a very long time, and wanting the food served wherever they are. How do you react?

Though you don't approve of it, do you let your children continue with their tantrums because of their illness?

It may often be that subconsciously, your child likes being ill because it ensures that you give them special treatment. Thus, here's what you need to do. Make sure you treat your children as normally as possible when they are ill. Of course, during such periods there is a need for more care, love and attention. But make sure that your children still follow the basic discipline.

SUMMARY OF CHAPTER 36/ VI

When children are sick, parents often struggle to balance compassion with discipline. While it's natural to feel concern, excessive worry can hinder recovery. Maintain normalcy in routines, enforce discipline, and provide love without allowing disruptive behaviors or excessive attention-seeking.

Secret No. 36

While it may be tempting to give your children extra special treatment when they're ill, resist the urge. Doing so may prolong their illness and delay their return to a normal routine.

37

THE SEVEN-DAY MENTAL UPLIFT

Hey parents, let me tell you about an amazing tool, which will help you have wonderful days of parenting. Tell me, has it struck you that once a parent, you are always a parent? Parenthood is irreversible. Do you want its path to be full of joy? I'm sure you do. Now, how many times have you thought to yourself, or told your friends, about parenthood 'It's so tough. It isn't that easy!' You must break this behaviour pattern to become a better parent!

This is an amazing tool that I use myself, to create new thoughts about things. Even while writing this I found it very useful. Whenever I feel overwhelmed and think that I have too much to do, this tool works like a miracle.

It's a MENTAL DIET!

It only lasts for seven days!

It is unbelievable how many things can be achieved in life with this tool!

For starters - you can be an amazing parent!

What must you do?

Starting from this moment, for the next seven days you must not allow any negative thoughts about parenthood to enter your mind. You must place a guard around your mind. You need to consciously check and filter the thoughts that enter your mind and only allow positive thoughts in.

Some of the thoughts you need to think about sifting out may be:

- Parenting is tough.
- I have sacrificed so many things in life because I am a parent.
- I don't know why I got into this.
- This is punishment.
- I didn't know what I was doing when I got into this, I'm stupid!
- I can't take this anymore! No more!!
- Children are brats.

These are some of the most common negative thoughts about parenting that I've come across.

If any of these thoughts wander into your head, then STOP! Start your seven days all over again. You must follow this mental diet for seven days continuously.

But be cool! Don't consciously tell your mind not to think any of these thoughts, because once you do that, I can guarantee that you will end up thinking only these! If I tell you not to think of a horrible red faced monkey, I know exactly what image will come to your mind instantly.

Decide firmly that you are going to follow this plan. If by chance you slip up, you have to start again. But, believe me, it will do wonders in your mind.

In the past, I have got piles of letters and emails from parents thanking me for introducing them to this amazing tool. If you go through the same amazing experience, do let me know as well. Let's create more effective parents together!

SUMMARY OF CHAPTER 37/ VI

Parents of teenagers, enhance your parenting with the MENTAL UPLIFT method. For one week, avoid negative thoughts about parenting and focus on positivity. If you catch negative thoughts, restart your week. This commitment nurtures your effectiveness as a parent. Share your transformative experiences with others as you grow together.

Secret No. 37

During the 'Seven Day Mental Diet,' do not let any negative thoughts about parenting enter your mind. If they do, restart your seven-day journey to reset your mindset.

38

BREAK THE PATTERN: FREAK OUT WITH YOUR CHILDREN – ONCE IN A WHILE.

What is the usual pattern of your weekday?

What time do you wake up? When do you eat?

What time do your children go to school/college?

When do they return? At what time do you have dinner?

When do you go to sleep?

What do you have for dinner most often?

You can have a fantastic time with your children by being a little spontaneous and playful once in a while. Consider occasionally saying:

- *"Let's skip homework and play a game!"*
- *"Let's make some funny noises together!"*
- *"Let's jump around the living room together!"*

I'm sure you can easily think of these activities. But is your weekend routine just as predictable as your weekdays? Sticking to a routine makes life dull. When the morning starts, you already know how the day will unfold - it's just another day. A little unpredictability makes life more exciting. While not necessary every day, surprises are essential from time to time. Do you ever take an unexpected break from your usual activities to enjoy some fun? When was the last time you went to a theme park, visited a zoo, or watched a movie with your children? Ensure you plan such outings at least once a month.

Like try to Dance together to a jazzy, upbeat song! I'm sure you can think of many more fun activities. No matter how silly they may seem, why not give them a try? It's a wonderful way for you and your children to bond and enjoy yourselves together. Changing up the routine can help strengthen your connection.

SUMMARY OF CHAPTER 38/ VI

Weekdays often involve set wake-up times, meals, school drop-offs, and dinners. To break monotony, incorporate spontaneous, playful activities with children. Consider outings monthly for unexpected fun and bonding, enhancing connections through varied experiences and silly activities.

Secret No. 38

Living with a set routine can lead to boredom. As a parent, occasionally shake things up and surprise your children, letting them escape their daily life. In those joyful, free moments, you'll be laying the foundation for a strong, lasting bond with them.

39

WHEN ARE YOU GOING TO VISIT AN ORPHANAGE?

Many a times in the past our organizations have organized visits of participants to orphanages. So,when we visit the orphanage we share them some incredible success tips and accelerated learning strategies.

Throughout the day, these children get to interact with the children who accompany us. The orphanages advise us not to ask about the children's backgrounds, as this could be painful, and the children we take them with, follow this.

These visits are some of the most rewarding experiences of my life. I always feel great energy, and I carry it until our next visit. The young ones in the orphanage yearn deeply for human connection, a hug, or a cuddle, something many have not experienced in a mother's arms. They rush for hugs and hold on tight.

Over time, I've seen that the kids we bring to visit orphanages learn the most. They gain valuable insights about life. When your children visit, they encounter a new reality, often realizing they've taken things like love, food, education, and more for granted.

Meeting orphans, especially babies, encourages them to ask, "Why them and not me?" This understanding makes them see how lucky they are, surrounded by opportunities and support and encourages them to use these wisely to lead meaningful lives.

Visiting an orphanage is a powerful experience that you shouldn't prohibit taking your children. Not only do the orphans benefit, but you and your children also gain a lot from this experience. Visiting can have a lasting impact.

Make plans to visit an orphanage with your children soon. Spend time there and help your children appreciate the blessings they have. This experience fosters compassion and humility, helping them grow into caring adults.

SUMMARY OF CHAPTER 39/ VI

When we conduct awareness walks and visit orphanages, share success tips, These visits enrich both orphans and our children, promoting gratitude and compassion. Engaging with orphans profoundly impacts perspectives, encouraging meaningful lives. Plan a visit soon.

Secret No. 39

Take your children to visit places such as an orphanage where others are less fortunate. This fosters gratitude and a deeper appreciation of their own blessings.

40

EXCESSIVE SLEEPING IS NOT A DISEASE BUT A SYMPTOM

Let me share one of my experiences with you.

I came across the parents of a fifteen-year-old girl. Their biggest problem was that their daughter sleeps a lot. This is what they told me. `On school days if you allow her, she sleeps till the very last minute. There are days she refuses to get up, and bunks school. Holidays are the worst. She can sleep continuously for even fifteen-sixteen hours. She wakes up, spends time in taking her bath, eating her food, watching TV and again, in few hours, she can go off to sleep. You just cannot believe it! On holidays we don't disturb her much because she might he really tired and we let her enjoy taking rest. What should we do? Because of this habit she even avoids meeting friends, scores very poorly in all subjects and never finishes school work on time.

Once or twice we even got complaints from some of the teachers that she looks very sleepy in the class and sometimes even sleeps off during the class. We even took her to a doctor as one of our friends suggested, it may be some kind of a `sleeping disorder'.

She has been under medication for a while and it has not helped her much. What will help our child come out of this?'

What will help the child get rid of this habit? Excessive sleeping is nothing but a symptom. A symptom for lack of motivation and lack of drive! When your children don't have anything interesting or exciting to do, then they choose to sleep. Over a period of time it becomes an addiction. They prefer sleep to doing anything else. Sleep is an addiction. If you sleep for long hours, you feel like sleeping for even longer! No medication can help.

Children must set motivational goals to break this habit, motivational goals for studies and for life. What are motivational goals? Ones that will make the child jump out of the bed as they wake up in the morning. Ones that will keep them awake for late hours in the night on certain days. Mindset like, 'I will pass in all subjects' versus that of 'I will be the most enthusiastic learner in my class!' Which will motivate your children? Obviously, the latter. The only way to help your children come out of excessive sleeping, is setting highly motivational goals.

The people who achieve a lot in their life, usually find little time to sleep. I personally know people who sleep for only four hours a day and still remain highly energetic and active throughout the day. I keep learning from them and make my sleep time shorter, while taking care not to cause any harm to my health.

If you want your children to sleep right, and be more active, ensure they have exciting goals to look forward to in life.

SUMMARY OF CHAPTER 40/ VI

Parents of a 15-year-old girl are worried about her excessive sleeping, affecting her social life and academics. The issue stems from a lack of motivation rather than a sleep disorder. Establishing inspiring goals can help children become more active and engaged.

Secret No. 40

Involved and thrilling goals can help your children develop a natural tendency to be energetic, reducing their need to oversleep.

41

NO BLAME, NO EXCUSES, NO COMPLAINTS

When you ask a child, 'Why did you get such low marks in science?' The child could say, 'I had very little time, and there was much to cover.'

Does this sound familiar? It's very easy to offer excuses, and blame somebody else for our failures, isn't it? Who sets up this pattern in the children's mind? Usually their parents. Because children look up to their parents and watch what they do.

When the father comes late for an important event, blaming the traffic, or blaming the boss, that registers in their children's minds. If there is going to be heavy traffic, you must start off early!

When children see parents coming up with lots of excuses and complaints, because it's easy to do so, they follow the same pattern. They fail to take responsibility for what happens in their life. If they fail badly at school, they start making excuses like, 'I have a bad memory,' 'The subject isn't interesting,' or, 'Nobody helps me at home', etc.

They tend to blame everyone except themselves. They blame their teachers for not teaching them properly. They blame the exams for being too tough, and they blame their friends for calling them up so often.

When people make excuses and place blame on others, they lose control over their lives and become victims, feeling powerless and unlucky. Successful people, however, take responsibility for their lives, believing they are accountable for whatever happens. By acknowledging responsibility, they gain the power to change and improve their situations, regaining control and enabling them to seek strategies for improvement.

To illustrate the power of taking responsibility and turning adversity into purpose, let us look at the life of Terry Fox.

Terry Fox, an eighteen-year-old athlete, was unexpectedly diagnosed with Osteosarcoma, leading to the amputation of his right leg. Instead of succumbing to victimhood, Terry believed he had a greater purpose. Inspired by the suffering of fellow cancer patients, he decided to run a marathon across Canada to raise awareness and funds for cancer research, launching the "Marathon of Hope." His goal was to collect a one-dollar donation from every Canadian, aiming for a total of one million dollars. Initially unnoticed and even criticized as seeking sympathy due to his exposed prosthetic leg, Terry persisted. Over time, his marathon gained significant attention and support, creating a nationwide movement.

He ran for 143 days, covering 3339 miles. Then, he was forced to stop, as his cancer had spread to his lungs. Shortly after this, he paced away. He managed to bring in over 26 million dollars as funds against the planned one million for cancer research. The Marathon of Hope, even today, takes place in many countries. Over 400 million dollars to date have been raised in Terry's name for cancer research.

SUMMARY OF CHAPTER 41/ VI

Children often learn to make excuses from their parents, who model behaviors of blame and responsibility avoidance. When parents justify their shortcomings, children internalize those patterns, leading them to fault others for their failures, such as poor school performance. In contrast, successful individuals accept responsibility, empowering themselves to effect change. Terry Fox exemplifies this, turning his cancer diagnosis into purpose by launching the "Marathon of Hope," which raised millions for cancer research and inspired a lasting movement.

Secret No. 41

Teach your children the powerful practice of taking responsibility for one's own life since that gives one the power to make changes. No Blame, No Excuses, No Complaints — should be one of your family's favourite adages.

42

TIME TO SAY 'I LOVE YOU'

How often do you express the love you feel towards your children?

LOVE — this four-letter word can create magic in your relationship with your children. Let me share a story with you. There was a teacher who, following the pmcess developed by Helice Bridge, started giving a blue ribbon to all the students at the end of their education, which said, 'Who I are makes a difference.'

She used to explain to them that the presence of every student made a difference to the course and even told them, how. Once, she decided to give three ribbons to each student and asked them to give these to people who they thought had made a difference to their life.

One of the students, who was doing a part-time job, gave the ribbon to his boss, to show his appreciation for the help his boss had given him and also gave him, the two remaining ribbons, asking him to offer them to someone who had made a difference to his life. The boss was really touched and on his way back home, thought about whom he could pass on the next two ribbons.

As he approached home, he noticed that the light in his son's room was still on, and he went to his room and told him 'I've been complaining about you all the time, as you haven't been doing well at school. But tonight I want to tell you that I love you and although I'm not able to spend much time with you, you've made a lot of difference in my life and I want you to accept this ribbon as a token of love from me.'

Listening to this the son burst into tears. The man asked his son whether he had hurt him, and his son replied, 'No, Dad. It was just that I was planning to kill myself as I thought that you didn't love me. I had planned to commit suicide tonight. Now all that has changed.' That was a magical moment in the boy's life.

We can also create magical moments in the lives of our children by doing small things that they will cherish. For example, you can surprise your children by giving your children something they would really love to have, not as a reward for doing something, but as an expression of your love. It can be even a small thing like an 'I love you' note in the lunch box with their favourite dishes. Or taking the whole family for a movie that the children would love to watch.

SUMMARY OF CHAPTER 42/ VI

Expressing love to children can create magical moments in their lives. One teacher used blue ribbons to highlight impact, leading a boss to share love with his son, who felt unwanted. Simple gestures, like notes or surprises, can profoundly affect children, strengthening the bond and showing that they matter.

Secret No. 42

Consciously create magical moments by showing your love and declaring it!

CHAPTER VII

SELF-DISCIPLINE AND RESPONSIBILITY

The goal of "Self-Discipline and Responsibility" is to give kids the routines, attitude, and accountability they need to grow up to be self-sufficient, resilient, and proactive adults. This chapter combines useful tactics with thoughtful advice for parents to help their kids develop self-management and responsibility.

Self-control and accountability are vital life skills that enable kids to overcome obstacles, accomplish their objectives, and make constructive contributions to their families and communities. Parents help children lay the groundwork for success and well-being throughout their lives by cultivating these traits through encouraging direction and practical application.

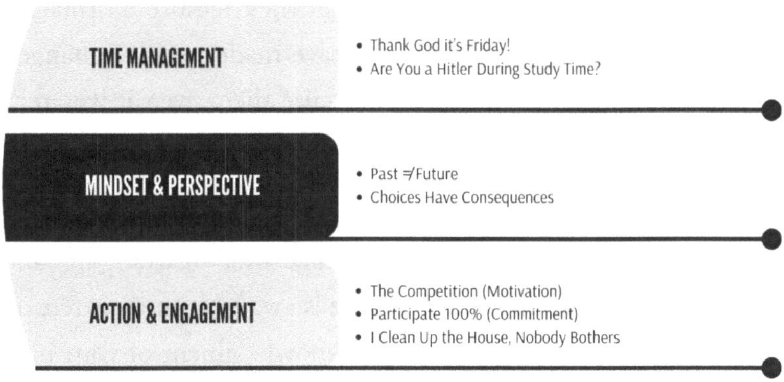

43

I CLEAN UP THE HOUSE, NOBODY BOTHERS

In our programs, children are highly motivated and committed to making positive changes in their lives. They come up with plans, embrace empowering beliefs, and learn effective strategies. However, some parents doubt these positive changes because they believe such improvements don't last. Even if their children come back home more focused and behaving differently, these parents do not recognize the change. Instead, they quietly watch and think, "Will these changes last?"

However, what children need most during this time is recognition and appreciation from their parents. They require affirmation that they are indeed different and have made positive changes. Parents often ask me, "Should we praise them even if we aren't fully convinced of their change?" I always respond, "Yes, praise them if you want the changes to last,"

Imagine this: You spend considerable time rearranging and tidying your home while your spouse is away. Upon their return, they notice nothing and offer no acknowledgment of your hard work. How would that leave you feeling? Would you feel inclined to make the same effort again?

The same principle applies at work. If you've gone beyond your usual duties but receive no appreciation or acknowledgment from your boss, your motivation might decline. You may question whether such effort is worth it in the absence of recognition.

Children require encouragement and affirmation just as adults do. Recognizing their efforts reinforces their growth. Praise cultivates persistence; silence signals neglect or dissatisfaction, prompting them to revert to old habits. Children need to see your belief in their commitment to change. With it, sustaining those changes becomes possible. To create lasting positive change and recognize and encourage their first steps. Show your children you approve of their efforts and show them that you completely believe in them. If you don't believe in your children's commitment to change, how can you expect them to change?

SUMMARY OF CHAPTER 43/ VII

Children need recognition and praise from parents to sustain positive changes in their lives. Without acknowledgment, they may feel discouraged and revert to old habits. Affirming their efforts fosters growth and belief in their commitment, reinforcing the importance of support for lasting change.

Secret No. 43

Appreciate your children's efforts if you want the positive change in them to become lasting.

44

THANK GOD IT'S FRIDAY!

"Thank god, It's Friday!!" Why Do My Children Feel This Way?

How do you approach your work? Considering you're awake for around sixteen hours each day, you spend at least eight hours at your job and over ten hours engaged in work-related activities. The majority of your active life revolves around work. If you equate weekends with freedom, does that imply you feel trapped during the weekdays?

Stop and think-this isn't just about your life. Are you passing on the same feeling about your work to your children? Do you feel incredibly happy on a Friday? How many times have you told your children this? 'Wow! the weekend's here!' If you wonder why your children feel a bit low on Monday mornings, it's because you feel the same way when you feel enthusiastic only at weekends and feel that your work is a pain, by expressing that to your children, you create the same mindset in them.

When are you going to say: 'Wow! I am going to work!' When is your child going to hear that? Create a powerful mindset. Let the next generation do their work with more passion. Stop saying TGIF to yourself and also to your children.

Start loving, your work right now and it will reveal a whole new attitude in yourself. Or choose some work that you are passionate about. Stop saying 'TGIF.'

Sometimes, parents ask me if this means that you must not have lots of fun activities during the weekend. NO! That isn't what I mean. But don't treat the weekend as the only time when you can have fun!

Be positive, and you'll find that – Your work can be your passion. Your work can be fun. Your work can make you feel great.

SUMMARY OF CHAPTER 44/ VII

Parents often express relief on Fridays, unintentionally transmitting a negative perception of work to their children. This mindset can lead kids to dread Mondays, mirroring their parents' attitudes. Instead, parents should foster enthusiasm for work, encouraging children to see it as a passion, not a burden. Providing recognition and affirmation to children is crucial for their growth and motivation. By believing in their efforts, parents can inspire lasting positive change and a healthier view of work.

Secret No. 44

Love your work. Or work on something you love. Your example will leave an imprint on your children's psyche. As a parent you must remember that through your children you're building the future generation & let that generation do their work with more passion.

45

PAST ≠ FUTURE

With each new sunrise we are given the opportunity to start afresh and make a new life for ourselves. No matter how many things may have gone wrong for you up to this day in your life, if you're willing to, you can start over and put all the negative events behind you. The past will not be the same as the future, provided you are willing to change. This is a very important fact that you must remember for effective parenting. Maybe your children are doing poorly at school. Or maybe you think that your children are not capable enough to do very well. But keep your spirits high. It does not mean that the future will not bring good tidings. Let me give you some examples.

Albert Einstein, one of the world renowned scientists was able to speak only after the age of four. He was able to read only when he crossed the age of seven. Many thought he was mentally retarded. His teachers thought he couldn't learn anything and hence expelled him from the school. Isaac Newton, the scientist who invented modern day physics, was very poor at maths in school. Agatha Christie, one of the world's best known authors and mystery writes, was identified as dyslexic. She struggled to learn to read as a child. Henry Ford, who started The Ford Motor Compauy, never made it through high school.

In spite of all their problems at school during their childhood, these people made something meaningful out of their lives.

All of us can achieve what we want for ourselves, only if we believe that we can!

If your children are having attitudinal or behavioural problems, do something about it right now It doesn't necessarily mean that they will continue to act in the same way in the future. And make sure that your children also realise this fact. Once children start believing that the future will not be the same as the past, things will start changing fast. Several times I have come across children who started living differently after being convinced that 'the Past is not to be Equated with the Future'. Although they might have got low marks in the past, they understand that they can still get one hundred per cent in maths now and work as a scientist in future, which is their dream. This prompts them into taking action towards improving their skills in that subject. There's a saying, that we are where we came from. I completely disagree. It does not matter in the least, if where you came from was not `great'! You can go anywhere you want to in the course of life, from there.

The paths of life are longer than we might think they are during moments of depression. So never think that the past and what is behind you, will be exactly mirrored in the future. It is always possible to turn over a new leaf, and live life anew, discover greener pastures and deeper sunsets, even if there were no promises of these in your past. Pass on this profound faith to your children.

SUMMARY OF CHAPTER 45/ VII

Each new day offers a fresh start, allowing you to leave negativity behind. Past struggles don't determine future success, examples like Einstein and Ford highlight this. Address children's behavior issues without fear; understanding that their future can differ from their past encourages transformation and resilience. Belief fuels their dreams and potential.

Secret No. 45

Teach your children that their past doesn't dictate their future and that failures are simply stepping stones to greater achievements.

46

ARE YOU A HITLER DURING STUDY TIME?

There is a family of four: the parents, a son, and a daughter, enjoying a holiday together. This is how the day looks through the eyes of the little boy. He gets up late in the morning, sees his mother's smiling face, freshens himself up, and has a leisurely breakfast. They decide to go for a drive. The father cleans the car and calls the children to join him. Both of them gladly agree. While cleaning, the father tells them how his father used to clean the car for hours together and how the aroma of his mother's food made them sneak inside and finish the delicious food, only to listen to her yelling at them later! The children enjoy the story, and the boy feels very close to his dad.

Suddenly, his sister decides to spray water on him with the hose. He gets drenched, pulls the hose from her, and starts spraying her in return. Then, they have some nice hot chocolate prepared by the mother and go out for a long drive to the woods. During the trip, Mother keeps cracking jokes, and they play some nice music. On the way back, they stop at their favorite restaurant, have a nice lunch, and return home. After their return, they decide to play the boy's favorite game, and all four of them are in it. The boy loses the game a couple of times and starts feeling bad. So they decide to cheer him up, and Mother helps him win the next game.

Around six o'clock in the evening, the mother asks the child, 'Did you finish your homework?' The child says, 'No.' Then the father yells, `Study time,' and the whole scene changes. The radio that was playing merrily throughout the day was switched off. The TV is also turned off. The house that was roaring with laughter a short while ago is very silent now as if something serious has happened. Father settles down on the sofa, reading the newspaper with a severe look. There is no smile on the mother's face either. The boy's sister sits at the study table quietly and does some work.

Even their dog sits noiselessly under the sofa. Everything looks gloomy. The child feels thirsty and asks permission from the mother to get up for a glass of water. Mother starts yelling at him, 'Whenever you sit down to do your homework, you feel thirsty or want to go to the toilet!' She isn't the same loving mother anymore. She looks furious. What kind of impression do you think your child will get? The same people who were so nice and loving just a while before have turned into tyrants, and the whole change of atmosphere conveys the idea that studying is something very serious. Something that makes the whole house turn into some kind of a horror movie. If a child at such a tender age feels that studying can never be enjoyed, will he ever get to like his studies? He starts hating his studies, and he can never associate it with fun. And who creates this feeling? Think about it. Can you change the whole scenario and create a feeling in your child that studying is actually fun?

You can only become good at things you truly enjoy. You can continue to be nice to your children but be firm about them completing the homework. You can also sit with your children and crack some jokes to lighten the atmosphere.

SUMMARY OF CHAPTER 46/ VII

A family of four enjoys a holiday, where the son experiences a joyful morning with his mother before a car-cleaning session with his father, who shares nostalgic stories. The day continues with fun activities, like playful water fights and a long drive filled with laughter. However, upon returning home, the atmosphere shifts drastically when homework time arrives. The mother becomes strict, and the once cheerful environment turns gloomy, making studying seem serious and unapproachable, leading the child to associate homework with negativity. A suggestion is made to create a more enjoyable studying atmosphere.

Secret No. 46

Isn't it true that only when you start loving and enjoying what you do will you become good at it? Make study time fun and exciting for your children so they enjoy their studies as much as they enjoy playing.

47

CHOICES HAVE CONSEQUENCES

All the choices we make in our lives have consequences. It's very important for children to realise this. Consequences help children understand the connection between what they do and what happens as a result of their actions. Consequences help children take responsibility of their actions, whether good or not-so-good. Most of negative behaviour displayed by children, is due to a lack of this understanding. If you don't let your children make decisions early in life, and you keep deciding for them, the consequence will be that they will lack the skills to take decisions and will never get the opportunity to learn. They get into a mindset where they blame others, and say things like, 'My father told me to do it, that's why it happened' or 'I told you that I wasn't interested, you made me do it.' They never understand the importance of the consequences of their actions, because you made the choices, on their behalf not by them. Sometimes children make certain decisions that don't go down too well with their parents. If their decision don't hurt anyone, and aren't illegal or unethical, let your children make the choice and learn from it.

However tempted you are to decide on their behalf, DON'T. Suppose a child wants to buy an expensive game using all her pocket money, let her buy it, but not before you tell her that she won't get any extra money from you later the same month. She will play with it once or twice and afterwards she may start feeling bored with it. She may not have enough money for any other activities, which she normally does. At that time, she will realise the consequence of her decision and learn from it. This was my experience with a family of three : father, mother and their fifteen-year-old son. The son was facing an exam in four or five months time and also wanted to take up extra cricket coaching, as his dream was to become a great cricket player.

His parents were worried that the extra coaching would affect his performance in the upcoming exam. There was a lot of discussion and argument between them regarding whether he should take up the coaching or not. The boy was prepared to listen to his parents, but was visibly upset at being told not to take up the coaching. I understood that if his parents stopped him from taking up the coaching, that would affect him even worse, as far as his studies were concerned. So finally, after a one and half hour session based on my thoughts, the parents made the following choice: They decided to let their son go ahead, but not before they made it very clear what consequences he would have to face.

They sat down with him and explained the advantages and disadvantages he would have, because of this decision. They described the possible outcomes of the option and told him clearly, `Now the CHOICE is YOURS.' I heard a sense of relief in their words. He started thinking and replied wisely, I'm so glad that you're my parents. I love you for putting your trust in me. I will take up the coaching and will make sure that I do really well in my exams. I know it's my choice!'

This was a special day for that family. The parents were creating a child who would become more responsible for the decisions he makes. I was very sure that the boy was learning how to make important decisions in his life, thereby establishing a pattern for future decision making. Let me share another incident with you.

The mother of one of the children who attended our programme was facing problems because her son wasn't keeping his room tidy. She found it very difficult to enter the room as it was filled with books and clothes. When she came to me asking for ideas on how to resolve the situation, she mentioned that her son had been pestering her to buy him a mobile phone. She went back home, sat down with him, and agreed on a win-win situation. She told him that she would buy him a mobile phone and let him use it but he had to pay for the top up.

She told him if he decided to keep his room clean and presentable, he would get some money as a mobile allowance every day, which would be kept in a box and given to him at the end of the month. Initially, this worked very well because the son wanted the mobile phone and was really enthusiastic about keeping his room clean. For a few months, everything went well. Then slowly the room started looking messy again. Mother kept her calm, in spite of the temptation to nag about it. She understood that if she started to nag, it would become her problem.

At the end of the month, there was very little money for her son's mobile phone allowance. He offered lots of excuses about why he wasn't able to keep his room clean, but both his parents were firm and he couldn't complain because he realised that the choice he made about the way he would spend his time, may not have been the best. It wasn't long before he began to take a much greater interest in keeping his room clean!

Let your children make their own choices, then allow them to face the consequences. As long as the situation is well under control, do not intervene to bail them out. Let them learn their lessons on their own.

All choices have consequences, and children need to recognize this connection to understand responsibility. Negative behavior often stems from a lack of awareness about the effects of their actions. If parents make decisions for their children, they risk instilling a mindset that blames others. Allowing children to make choices, even if they lead to mistakes, fosters growth. For example, a child who spends pocket money on a game might learn to feel the consequences later. In another case, a boy was allowed to pursue cricket coaching while being made aware of exam implications, leading to responsible decision-making. A mother solved her son's messy room issue by linking mobile phone privileges to cleanliness, which taught him accountability. Ultimately, children should face the outcomes of their decisions to learn valuable life lessons independently.

SUMMARY OF CHAPTER 47/ VII

All choices come with consequences, and children must understand this connection to foster responsibility. Often, negative behaviors arise from a lack of awareness of their actions' effects. If parents always make decisions for their children, it can lead to blame-shifting rather than accountability. Allowing children to make choices, even if they make mistakes that promotes essential growth. For instance, a child spending pocket money on an expensive game may soon realize the repercussions of that decision. Similarly, a boy who was permitted to follow his cricket aspirations, while understanding the potential impact on his studies, learned valuable decision-making skills. A mother tackled her son's untidy room by tying his mobile phone privileges to his cleanliness, which cultivated a sense of responsibility. Ultimately, it is crucial for children to experience the consequences of their choices, enabling them to learn important life lessons independently.

Secret No. 47

Let your children make their own choices, then allow them to face the consequences. As long as the situation is well under control, do not intervene to bail them out. Let them learn their lessons on their own.

48

THE COMPETITION

In on on the competitions for children I happened to watch the backstage. I witnessed numerous parents becoming overly anxious as they urged their children to perform. Dressed for the competition, many kids resisted their parents' requests, with some crying or stopping mid-song.

For instance, one mother pleaded with her daughter, 'Come, sing your song one last time.' Her daughter, about five or six years old, said, 'Mom, I want some water.' The mother gave her some water. After her drink, the child resisted singing, looking here and there and everywhere, saying, 'I will sing later, Mom!' The mother started crying. 'Please do it now; you have very little time!' The reaction from the child was a perplexed look. What has happened to my mother — why is she crying? This led to fear, and the child immediately started singing in a low tone filled with fear!

I also observed various parental behaviors, such as some parents treating their children like royalty and their body language suggesting they had unconsciously taken on a role of servitude. Others promised lavish rewards, saying, "If you perform well, I'll buy you anything you want," which seemed to alleviate the children at the moment. However, this approach fails to instill a sense of personal responsibility or an understanding that the competition is theirs to own.

After the performance, a shift occurred, parents became strict, some dragging their children away with a sense of relief. This inconsistency sends mixed messages to children.

What will a child understand from this?

Children understand that parents try to control their activities using insidious means until they perform. Reading this behavior, they feel that the parents are highly manipulative, and they, too, wait for the next opportunity to take control.

SUMMARY OF CHAPTER 48/ VII

After a group song competition, I observed anxious parents pressuring their children to perform, leading to resistance and distress. Various parental behaviors, like offering rewards, conflicted with strictness afterward, confusing children about control and responsibility in performances, fostering manipulative relationships.

Secret No. 48

Instead of making competition days into stressful days, why don't you treat your children normally? Allow them to participate in the experience, not just for the prize. The prizes make sense only if they aim and strategize to win. They have to do this for themselves, or those prizes are not for them but for you

49

PARTICIPATE 100%

Have you ever heard of the widespread practice of Zen? Zen is a form of Buddhism that emphasizes moment-by-moment awareness and seeing deeply into the nature of things through direct experience.

Simply put, Zen teaches you to experience every moment of your life. The Japanese link this philosophy beautifully with a special tea ceremony. The ceremony has three stages. The first comprises the purification of the utensils to be used. Next comes serving the tea, and finally, the utensils are purified and put away. Each stage is elaborate, and the guest and the host must participate fully in all of them. This tea ceremony is harmonious with the Zen concept of living fully in the present.

I introduce the concept of Zen here because it's very important for children to participate fully in whatever activity they are doing. It's when they do this they get the best results. Children must understand that to get the desired results, they must give their best effort. It's not a matter of putting in 50% effort for 50% results; it's more of an all-or-nothing process: either you get the results you want, or you get nothing. If even one child doesn't give their best effort in a football match, there is a chance that the team may lose the game.

Once children show 100% commitment, they will be willing to do whatever it takes, no matter how uncomfortable or complicated the task.

To support this, let me share the story of a boy with you.

A boy was fascinated by the circus. He visited it as often as possible and was particularly captivated by rope walking. The person who walked on the rope performed this dangerous task with considerable ease despite the absence of a net to catch him if he fell. The boy considered the rope walker his hero and asked him for the secret behind his success.

The man said, "I see every walk as the most important walk of my life, and I want it to be the best. I carefully plan every walk—from what I wear to what I eat and look like. I rehearse each walk mentally and physically, and when I'm up on the rope, I clear my mind and focus all my attention on what I'm doing."

SUMMARY OF CHAPTER 49/ VII

Zen, emphasizes awareness of the present through firsthand experience. Its concepts are evident in a Japanese tea ceremony, highlighting complete involvement in every phase. Kids ought to put forth their utmost effort in tasks; this all-or-nothing mindset achieves the intended outcomes. A boy understands from a tightrope walker to regard each step as vital, concentrating fully on his work.

Secret No. 49

100% commitment. You display it as a parent, and your children will learn your secret.

CHAPTER VIII

RELATIONSHIPS AND SOCIAL SKILLS

"Relationships and Social Skills," addresses the evolving landscape of children's and teenagers' relationships with parents, siblings, friends, and teachers highlighting the importance of connection, empathy, and healthy communication for social and emotional development.

Strong relationships and social skills are built through empathy, respect, and consistent, open communication. By modeling positive connections, validating children's experiences, and providing guidance without judgment, parents can help children and teens navigate the complexities of friendships, sibling dynamics, and family bonds laying the foundation for lifelong social and emotional well-being.

PARENT-TEEN RELATIONSHIPS

- Communication Challenges
- Must Parent Go Into Coma?
- Watch A Movie With Children

SIBLING & PEER RELATIONSHIPS

- Why Do My Children Consider Their Siblings to be Their 'Biggest Enemies?
- Teenagers Find Their Friends More Understanding
- Children Hate Comparisons

SELF EXPRESSION

- What Your Children Want to Say About Friends and Teachers?
- What Your Children Want to Say About You?

50

MUST PARENTS GO INTO A COMA?

I recently worked with a celebrity couple who were very worried about their teenage daughter. They came in looking upset, saying, "We don't know what to do. Our daughter ignores us; her friends, especially boyfriends, seem to matter more. We're at a loss." The father agreed, expressing doubt about their parenting. When I turned to him, he told me, 'We are in the worst phase of our lives. If you know who we are, you'll realize that we're busy artists, and now we're wondering if we have made a huge mistake somewhere. Haven't we guided our daughter along the right path? Because of her behavior, we fight with one another almost daily. We're rich enough and even prepared to drop our careers to do something about our daughter's life. But is that the solution?'

The mother was almost in tears, worrying she hadn't done her job as a parent. She told me how her daughter often left home early, stayed out late, and sometimes didn't even come back home at night. She was convinced that , Once children become teenagers, their parents must go into a COMA and return to their senses only when the child becomes twenty-one! But now I wonder if that's working.'

The idea shocked me. I asked how long they had been in this "coma" mindset, and she said for four years since their daughter turned 12. They had stopped asking about her life to give her space, but that only widened the gap. The daughter stopped communicating with them, and her behavior got more concerning.

I told them, "Don't disengage as she grows. She needs you more than ever. That 'coma' approach leaves your child feeling alone. Kids might seem to prefer talking to friends, but they need your understanding and presence."

SUMMARY OF CHAPTER 50/ VIII

A worried celebrity couple sought help for their teenage daughter, feeling disconnected and doubting their parenting. They expressed fears about her behavior and their own relationship struggles. I advised them not to disengage, emphasizing the importance of their presence and understanding during this critical phase.

Secret No. 50

Never disengage from active involvement in your children's lives, even as they are about to enter the 'teenage years' – never 'go into a coma.' Remember, they need you more during these emotionally challenging years.

51

TEENAGERS FIND THEIR FRIENDS MORE UNDERSTANDING THAN THEIR PARENTS!

NONSENSE! Who said so? The teen years are the ones in which children want to show that they're mature enough to handle things by themselves. They want to be treated as adults. They need to feel confident about their feelings, and their ways of doing things. As a parent, if you don't attribute any importance to these feelings, you'll not be very successful. The teenagers would then turn to their friends for help. Their friends respond to them in a way that makes them believe that their feelings are important.

Say, for example, your daughter is worked up because she hasn't received a phone call she was expecting from one of her friends. If she shares her feelings with you, how will you tend to react? Most parents will say. So what? Forget it and carry on with what you're doing. Whenever children face this kind of reaction they feel that their parents don't understand their feelings.

Connect with your teenager's feelings. You probably think that that call is not of paramount importance. It may be a call just to decide if they want to go for a newly released movie or not! But you need to understand what your children feel. To them, the friend not calling up, might even signal a rejection or exclusion. So, always be sensitive to your teenager.

Some things you can do with your teenage children are:

Hang out!

Just hang out with them. Few parents think of this and even fewer do it. Hanging out isn't just a 'useless' way of spending time. It's about creating deeper connections with your children through the creation of a comfort level.

Connect with your children's feelings.

Make them feel important

Remember that they're no longer just kids who will always listen to what you say. They've already formed their own opinions about the world and feel certain things need to be done in a specific way. They may or may not be right. But what *you* think of as the right way may also not work. What is the key here Is for you to respect their thoughts and ideas. When making family decisions such as arranging a trip or buying a household item, ask them for their suggestions. Your child needs to be part of these important decisions.

Give a hug and kiss, but not in public

When did you last hug or kiss your children? Many parents stop once their children reach the age of seven or eight. Whatever age your children are, they still need affection though they may not always show it. At the other extreme are parents who overdo it, and display their affections in front of others. Teenagers hate this - do you know why? Because it makes them look like children in front of others - especially in front of their friends. Whatever age your children are, they need that hug and kiss from you.

SUMMARY OF CHAPTER 51/ VIII

Teenagers seek independence and validation for their feelings, needing parents to acknowledge their emotions. Dismissing their concerns can lead them to seek support from friends, who often validate them. For instance, if a teen feels anxious about not receiving a call, parents should recognize its significance rather than trivialize it. Building connections through activities, involving them in family decisions, and showing affection appropriately are essential for fostering trust and understanding during this critical development stage.

Secret No. 51

Parents understand that teenagers often turn to friends because they find their emotions mirrored in them. However, this doesn't mean they no longer need you. Now is the time to take them seriously as young adults and strengthen your bond by spending more time with them to understand who they are truly.

52

WHY DO MY CHILDREN CONSIDER THEIR SIBLINGS AS THEIR ` BIGGEST ENEMIES'?

We train about several thousand children every year in various parts of the world. One of the statements that I have heard from children is, 'My biggest enemy in the world is my brother (or sister).' For some children, this feeling is intense; others say it is for fun. Parents often ask me how to manage the situation and stop their children from thinking of their sibling as a rival. ('Sibling rivalry' is a complex problematic term coined by Alfred Adler.) According to psychologists, if the children are closer in age and belong to the same sex, then the intensity of rivalry is higher. Makes no sense! I've seen many parents who have a similar idea about their children, too.

The fact is that when children have to share their parent's love and affection, at certain times, they may feel excluded and begin to believe that they get less attention because of their siblings. This phenomenon isn't only true between siblings. It's a natural feeling between any two human beings. As a parent, your first step should be never to assume that siblings will be rivals. When two humans live under the same roof and share the same resources, misunderstandings and a sense of competition are a natural part of life. Don't make the issue any bigger than it is.

Many parents think they must be fair, have the same rules and expectations, and provide the same opportunities to each of their children. However, what is most important is to be sensitive to each child's individual needs.

SUMMARY OF CHAPTER 52/ VIII

Rivalry often stems from sharing parental love. Parents shouldn't assume siblings will compete and should focus on each child's unique needs rather than strict fairness.

Secret No. 52

Each child is unique. So, instead of loving equally, learn how to Love Uniquely. Understand what is special about your children and love them for their unique selves. Do not make sibling rivalry any bigger than it is!

53

THE POWER OF HUMAN CONNECTION

There was a student in a class who was doing really well in his studies. He was extremely good at whatever he was doing and his parents and teachers were obviously happy with the way things were going. He scored extremely well in every test that he took.

Once his professor conducted a test and at the end asked an unusual question. He asked the students to write the name of the person who cleans the classroom every day.

In fact, the lady who cleaned the room often spent time with the children, serving them drinks, etc. This student couldn't answer the question and so was very upset with the professor. He went and asked the professor after the test why he had asked such a question which was totally unrelated to the subject. And he explained to the Professor that he'd spent a lot of time and effort preparing for the test!

After all those preparations he wouldn't get the top marks, just because of that one last question. Then the professor explained to him the importance of knowing the people around him and the fact that leading a meaningful life was not just about studies! It was after this incident that the student made efforts to understand the value of human relationships.

What have you learnt from this? You'll agree with me that no society can sustain itself unless, its members have learnt the sensitivities, motivations, and skills involved in assisting and caring for other human beings. However, schools today focus more on competition, than on care.

Tests compare one student's performance with that of other students, but schools never explain the importance of creating human connections.

That is why, as parents, you must ensure that your children realise how important this is. The emotional and intellectual development of children depend upon the deep and healthy relationships they develop in their early life.

SUMMARY OF CHAPTER 53/ VIII

A student excelled academically but struggled with a question about the classroom cleaner, highlighting his lack of awareness of people around him. The professor emphasized the importance of human relationships over mere academic success. Schools should encourage empathy, as children's emotional growth relies on healthy relationships alongside their studies.

Secret No. 53

Teach your children the value of relationships, guiding them to build deep, nurturing connections that enrich the soul.

54

WATCH A MOVIE WITH YOUR CHILDREN!

Which movie have you seen lately? I mean, with your children! How often do you watch movies together?

Most parents see it as a waste of time, and I often hear parents express, "Who wants to sit and watch a boring movie? Especially with my children, who keep asking me all sorts of questions about what's happening and why it's happening.'

The fact is that this is one of the best times to connect with your children and share things. Don't you think so? Movies create a great impact on the curious minds of children. They think that whatever's happening in the movie is true, and your presence and participation helps to create an even greater impact on their mind. Sharing thoughts about the movie, about certain characters, their morals and any number of things that you can talk about, will help your children develop certain positive beliefs about themselves. When they see that their parents share their beliefs, this will bring them closer to their parents.

However, it's important to identify the right kind of movie to watch together. There are certain movies with powerful messages, such as Lion King, Iqbal, Hanuman, Miracle worker, Finding Nemo, Moana and The Harry Potter series — you must watch them along with your children. Allow them to think about the films and discuss them. Build a movie library at home and reserve family time to watch them.

There are some wonderful things you can learn from Harry Potter, who can serve as a source of inspiration for your children. Although, JK Rowling has set the story in the backdrop of a magical world, Harry's inspirational character is someone who most children can relate to in one stay or the other. He may not be academically the most intelligent child in the class but he has his goal clearly laid out before him and makes every effort to achieve it. Harry's character commands a lot of respect and proves to be a great source of inspiration for the new generation of children, because of his honesty, courage. Moana is a character which displays courage, self-discovery, and empathy.

SUMMARY OF CHAPTER 54/ VIII

Watching movies with your children can be a meaningful bonding experience. Though some parents view it as time-wasting, films can positively impact children's beliefs and values. Engaging conversations about characters and themes from meaningful movies, like "Harry Potter," strengthen bonds and promote personal growth.

Secret No. 54

This one is a question. So, which film will you watch with your children this weekend?

55

CHILDREN HATE COMPARISONS

This is a common conversation at home between siblings. Seeing her son's messy room, a busy and tired mother starts yelling, "Why can't you keep your books organized? At your age, your brother John kept his room tidy alone." Hearing this repeatedly, the son becomes enraged and yells, "Why do you always compare me with John?"

Each child desires to be seen as unique with their own identity. They dislike being compared to others and deserve to be treated as individuals. Yet, many parents habitually compare their children to their siblings and friends. Interestingly, the same parents may later say, "Why do you depend on your brother so much? Why can't you do things independently?" This leaves the child confused, wondering, "What do my parents want from me?"

When children hear these comparisons, their self-esteem can diminish. Imagine they started comparing you: "If only my father were as loving as my friend John's father," how would that feel? It's no different for your child.Therefore, treat your children as unique individuals, offering them their goals and appreciation. Even when disciplining them, avoid comparisons with others. They dislike it, and truthfully, don't you as well?

SUMMARY OF CHAPTER 55/ VIII

A mother yells at her son for a messy room, comparing him to his brother. This leads to resentment, confusion, and diminished self-esteem. Children desire individuality and appreciation.

Secret No. 55

Treat your children as individuals. Do not compare them with others.

56

ELEVEN THINGS YOUR CHILDREN WANT TO SAY ABOUT FRIENDS AND TEACHERS AND WHAT YOU CAN LEARN FROM THEM

Often, parents cannot give due importance to their children's friends and see their importance in their children's lives. Very usually, parents blindly accept the teachers' views on what their children are like. The following are your children's views that you should remember to understand them better.

1. Do treat my friends well. They mean a lot to me.
2. I would like to spend quality time with my friends, as it helps me develop social skills.
3. Let me decide about going out on the trip with my friends! I need to learn to make decisions on my own.
4. Some of your displays of affection in front of them make me feel uncomfortable.

5. If I come home late, please don't conclude that my friends are bad! It may be because we had something more than usual to share on that day!
6. I'd love to invite my friends home for dinner! I know it is asking a lot from you, but let me help you. I'll do it with enthusiasm!
7. Sometimes, I'll complain about my teachers. Please don't join in with me, as that will only confirm what I am saying is correct.
8. Please understand that I don't listen to my teachers because I lack concentration; it's because I get distracted when the subject isn't interestingly taught.
9. Sometimes, when I don't answer the teacher for days, it isn't out of disinterest; it may be because I don't know the answer or I feel shy!
10. If my teacher says I am a slow learner, NEVER ACCEPT IT, PLEASE! Help me PROVE IT WRONG. Once you accept that I am a slow learner, as a fact, I'm going to end up being slow not only in my studies but also in life.
11. Help me understand that my teachers can be partial sometimes, as they can't always be fair to every student!

SUMMARY OF CHAPTER 56/ VIII

Parents often overlook the significance of their children's friends and their opinions. Children desire respect for friendships, quality time for social skills, autonomy in decisions, and understanding regarding teachers and learning. They seek support against negative labels and recognition of teachers' biases for better comprehension and self-confidence.

Secret No. 56

Understand the importance of your children's friends in their lives. Also, don't blindly accept teachers' views on your children's behavior and characteristics.

57

ELEVEN THINGS YOUR CHILDREN WANT TO SAY ABOUT YOU AND WHAT YOU CAN LEARN FROM THEM

These are your children's views about you, the parents:

1. It may appear as if I'm arguing with you sometimes, but that doesn't mean that I hate you or that I don't love you I'm just expressing my views, which are not the same as yours, on a particular subject!
2. You can be assertive and firm with me. That gives me confidence about your abilities and your skill to make decisions.
3. You needn't always be nice to me or else I may take you for granted and may start ignoring your advice.
4. I felt good when you asked me my ideas about painting the house. It made me feel an important part of the family
5. Sometimes I may hurt my siblings. It isn't that I hate them, it's just that I want your love as much as they do.

6. 1 would love to go and see some films with you. 1 enjoy discussing my ideas.
7. I would like to just sit and chat with you sometimes, it makes me feel more connected to you.
8. You keep telling me, 'If you get good grades in your exams, I will buy you a computer.' I start feeling that I'm studying for you!
9. When I broke the window, you told me that if I did it one more time I would get the spanking of a lifetime! Did you expect me to repeat it?
10. I broke an expensive crystal vase that you love, but you never said anything. I want you to express your feelings honestly, including when you disapprove of my behaviour or actions.
11. When I came running home to tell you about my football victory, you told me how sick and tired you were of washing my dirty shirts. Please join in my joy! I could be the next sports superstar.

SUMMARY OF CHAPTER 57/ VIII

Children express warmth and desire for connection with parents. They appreciate assertiveness, crave inclusivity, desire discussions, and want honest feedback on actions. While they seek love and acknowledgment, they also hope parents share joy in achievements rather than focus solely on issues, fostering a supportive environment.

Secret No. 57

Your children must respect you. Have the right balance between your love and strictness.

CHAPTER IX

POSITIVE DISCIPLINE AND BEHAVIOUR MANAGEMENT

"Positive Discipline and Behaviour Management," provides a framework for guiding children's behavior through empathy, clear expectations, and consistent, respectful strategies. The focus is on nurturing self-control, responsibility, and mutual respect moving away from punitive approaches toward methods that enhancing growth and connection.

Positive discipline is about guiding, not punishing. By combining kindness and firmness, setting clear expectations, and maintaining a strong parent-child connection, adults can help children develop self-discipline, empathy, and lifelong respect for themselves and others

UNDERSTANDING CHILD BEHAVIOR

- Your Children are Gifted
- The Power of Your Expectations
- Resistance Means Lack of Rapport

DISCIPLINARY TECHNIQUES

- Should You Scold Your Children?
- Is That Your Pattern?

PARENTING PHILOSOPHIES

- Beliefs About Parenting
- Power Of Words

58

YOUR CHILDREN ARE GIFTED

Are your children gifted?

There are parents who would immediately say, 'Yes!' However, there are parents who would think for a while before saying yes.

So, for people who are contemplating, Consider my question - Are your children gifted? That is, Are they gifted with

1. A lot of love and affection from your parents?
2. A quality education?
3. A framework of support in society?

The truth is only a handful number of children in the world experience all of these benefits in their lives. So, let me ask you once more: do you consider your children gifted? I'm confident that now your response is a going to be a strong YES!

Making your children understand that they're 'gifted' is vital. That is because, when you look at anyone who's reached their full potential early, you'll see it wasn't just their skills that launched them forward, but their deep internal realization that they are unique and gifted.

It's not just great talent that makes a child stand out. For instance, you might find a golfer with better skills than Tiger Woods somewhere in the world, but what makes Tiger Woods exceptional isn't just his talent but his awareness of being gifted.

What your children should be thinking is, "I must make my life meaningful. I must use every opportunity that comes my way." For some, life itself will show them how fortunate they are. Even as an adult, it's important to tell yourself, "I am gifted." Not because of wealth but because you wake up in good health and have opportunities to explore. Feeling thankful can lead to many things, such as:

- Is there a reason why things are going well in your life?
- Should you make each day even more meaningful and purposeful?
- Should you create a lasting impact on the world?

I'm sure you answered yes to all these questions. As a parent, it's your role to help your children realize this, too. This understanding greatly helps children become high achievers,

Teach your children to say, "I am gifted." Just as how you teach them table manners or why they shouldn't waste food. This will automatically aid in making the children realise that they are 'gifted'.

SUMMARY OF CHAPTER 58/ IX

Consider if your children are truly gifted. Giftedness includes love, quality education, and societal support, which few experience fully. Instilling a sense of being gifted is crucial for their growth.

Talents alone don't define exceptional individuals; awareness of their uniqueness does. Encourage your children to embrace their gifts and create meaningful lives to become high achievers.

Secret No. 58

Teach your children to understand and value the numerous benefits and talents they possess. Seeing themselves as 'gifted' can fundamentally shift their perception of the world.

59

THE POWER OF YOUR EXPECTATIONS

The expectations you have for your children are incredibly powerful. Let's do an exercise: Look around and note all the things you can see that are blue. If you want to take more time, look again and make sure that you note everything that is blue. Done? Now, close your eyes and recall things around you that are green. What happened? Why can't you list them? Now, that is because you expected me to ask you to recall all the blue things. Thus, you deleted all the stuff in other colors from your mindscape. You decided not to look at them. Remember, Your eyes only see what your mind wants you to see!

If you constantly think of your children as lazy or difficult, you'll only see that behavior. Parents often complain, "My child is always lazy!" To which I respond, "Always?".

The idea of a 'self-fulfilling prophecy' was introduced by sociologist Robert K. Merton, also known as the Pygmalion Effect. What is this Pygmalion Effect? According to Greek mythology, a Cypriot sculptor by the name of Pygmalion was able to, purely on the basis of his will and belief, bring life to a statue that he sculpted.

The fact that he was able to turn his expectations into reality is the reason why this phenomenon came to be known as the Pygmalion Effect. According to this phenomenon, 'what you expect is what you focus on, and the same will be the outcome.'

In one popular experiment by Dr. Rosenthal, students were told certain rats were smart, and others were not. The "smart" rats performed better in mazes simply because of the expectations set for them.

Are you unintentionally performing a similar experiment with your children through your expectations? Whether they are negative or positive, they shape behavior. "I know you'll spend all your time watching TV," which will likely result in children doing just that. If you want your kids to excel in math, treat them like geniuses in the subject. The same goes for any skill—they'll live up to the expectations you set.

Even for small habits, positive expectations can turn behavior into reality.

SUMMARY OF CHAPTER 59/ IX

Your expectations shape your children's behavior significantly. An exercise demonstrates how what you focus on influences perception. If you see your child as lazy, you notice only that behavior. The Pygmalion Effect shows that expectations can bring about corresponding outcomes. Positive expectations can help improve skills and habits, as illustrated by a child's progress when praised for neatness, showcasing how belief influences reality.

Secret No. 59

If you think: "My child is shy," they will become shy. Conversely, expect confidence, and you'll nurture a confident child. Your expectations should guide them positively. If you believe your children are untidy and lazy, that's what they'll be. If you see them as helpful and smart, they will become just that.

60

RESISTANCE MEANS A LACK OF RAPPORT

Here are snatches of a conversation between a boy and his mother:

`Switch off the TV right now and do your home work.' `Yes Mom, in just a few minutes.' After ten or fifteen minutes, the Mother comes back and yells, `How many times have I told you not to waste your time watching TV. You will go blind!' `I said that I'll switch it off. Why are you shouting so much? You never let me watch my programmes peacefully even for a few minutes. I know what I'm doing.'

And the conversation ends in intense negativity between the mother and the son. Sounds familiar? Check this out.

`John! Look at that mess. It looks like a fish market! When are you going to clean it up?' `I can't do it now, Dad. I'm busy. My room isn't that dirty anyway.' `What work do you have now?' `I have to meet my friend.' `Can't that wait? Cleaning is hardly going to take a few minutes.' i told you I will do it later. Leave me alone.'

`Do you know what I was doing at your age?' `Oh, you mean those old days. Times have changed now , It isn't the same.'

It goes on and on, and soon enough both start fuming at each other. Are there times when you wonder. Why do my children talk to me in this way? How come they talk back all the time? Why is there so much resistance from my children to whatever I say? The success of any person to person communication depends on the kind of rapport that exists between the people involved. How can you build a good rapport? If you know how to step into the model of your children's world, you will be the best parents for your children. Your children need to feel that you understand them. You need to understand how they feel about their school, friends, teachers, subjects, and about life in general. In order to build a good rapport with your children you have to learn to see what they see. The fact that one of your children's friends hasn't called up as promised, may be a bigger thing for your child, than a war between two countries, your switch to a new job or your boss threatening to fire you! But if you don't give due importance to such feelings, you aren't seeing what they see, and you will never be able to understand what goes on in their mind. Make quality time for your children — for their grievances, and listen to them. Then share your thoughts. Find a solution that works for both of you. I will share one of my experiences with you:

A girl was very keen to learn the piano. But her father was totally against it as he was afraid that she would not be able to give enough time to her studies. Consequently, the young artist was extremely upset. She felt that her father could never understand her 'He doesn't have any knowledge of music. He doesn't know that music can help me perform even better in ny exams.' Then we agreed on a plan of action. The mother sat with both of them to structure a win-win situation. The girl gave the following assurance to her mother, After joining piano classes, I will definitely either keep up my present grades or will score better.' The mother made the father accept the deal. And indeed, the girl kept her promise. In fact, she started scoring much higher than before, and a few months later her mother wept when she showed me a thank-you card that she had received from her daughter

So, before determinedly saying NO to what they ask, think for a moment. Why are your children asking for what they're asking? Are you missing out on something important by immediately denying it?

You don't have to say yes to everything your children ask of you, but before saying no, understand why they are asking for something. Allow them to take some risks; they may outperform your expectations. They will understand that you trust them and not to let you down. Learn your children's language and respect their way of thinking. That will go a long way in helping you build up a great rapport with your children, and wait and see, how easily the solutions will come!

SUMMARY OF CHAPTER 60/ IX

A conversation between a boy and his mother reveals tension when he resists doing homework, prioritizing TV instead. Similarly, John and his dad clash over cleaning his messy room. Both parents express frustration, questioning their children's defiance. This highlights a common struggle of parents feeling disconnected from their children. To bridge this gap, parents should strive to understand their children's perspectives, acknowledging their feelings and interests. Listening actively and finding compromises can lead to mutually beneficial solutions, fostering trust and connection. Before dismissing requests, consider the underlying reasons to strengthen the parent-child relationship.

Secret No. 60

Learn to appreciate your children's perspective and respect their thinking. This will greatly help you build a positive rapport. As solutions emerge naturally, you'll see possibilities in ways you hadn't before.

61

SHOULD YOU SCOLD YOUR CHILDREN?

Let as imagine a scenario at home, when the father returns home from work, sees his son watching TV, and gets angry with him. The conversation goes as follows:

Father (in a serious tone): 'Son, have you finished your homework?'

Son: 'No dad, I'll do it shortly.'

Father: 'When are your exams coming up?'

Son: 'I told you already, they are starting the day after tomorrow.'

Father (in an angry tone): 'So what are you doing right now? How many times have I told you to stop watching TV? Don't you know that it's a waste of time? Switch it off, go and start your studies right now!'

The son feels lousy and goes to his room, but will he really study? Look at this from the child's perspective. The child thinks. 'My father always behaves like this. Whenever he comes back from his office in a bad mood, he just shouts at me.' While such thoughts run through a child's mind, will he concentrate, even though he may have a book in his hand?

As a parent, when you see your children wasting time, it's natural to get angry and you sometimes end up scolding them, otherwise, you feel the children may continue acting the same way, which is not useful for them in the long run. But whenever you get angry and shout at the children, the children may see only the anger, but not the true cause of it.

When you shout at them in a rage, it's also very important for you to say why you am hurt, and express your fear about the consequences that they may have to face because of the behavior. Last but not least, never forget to show that you appreciate them and to say as often as you feel the need, that you love them.

It helps them understand that their parent is not angry with them as a person, but only with their behaviour and this is what will bring about positive changes in your children.

SUMMARY OF CHAPTER 61/ IX

A father returns home, sees his son watching TV, and scolds him for not finishing homework before exams. The son feels hurt as the father expresses anger without explaining the underlying concern. It's essential for parents to communicate feelings and show love, fostering understanding and encouraging positive behavioral changes in children.

Secret No. 61

If you shout or scream at your children as you scold them, valid as your grounds are, they may miss the real lesson you wish to impart. So, never simply scold; always give your reasons for doing so.

62

IS THAT YOUR PATTERN?

What you do has a huge impact on your children! I don't have to say this, as you already know it. This chapter is about a recent counselling experience of mine with a family.

A strong concern one parent shared with me was this, "Our daughter isn't sure of what she's doing and constantly seeks reassurance." The mother explained, "During exams, after handing in her papers, she frequently worries about things like whether her roll number is correct or if all the papers are pinned together properly. She often asks the teacher to check, which the teacher has mentioned to us."

Similarly, at home, the daughter repeatedly checks her school bag to ensure she has all her books. After completing tasks, she doubts whether she's done them correctly. I asked the mother, "Do you ever question whether you've turned off the gas stove or locked the door properly?" She admitted, "Sometimes I even return home halfway to check."

I pointed out the parallel behavior, and she said, "For me, it's OK because I'm older and forgetful, but my daughter is just fifteen!" This behavior isn't a memory issue; it's a behavioral pattern.

Patterns are routines we unconsciously develop, like starting our day with coffee and a newspaper. Often, they make us question, "Did I lock the house? Turn off the gas?" Children adopt these behaviors from their parents, for good or for bad.

To break such a pattern, create a memorable moment when completing a task. For example, after turning off the stove, you could jump and say, "I've shut it!" or mark a chart to keep track. Make it distinct so your brain remembers it as an event. Change up these memorable actions to reinforce the habit.

SUMMARY OF CHAPTER 62/ IX

A parent expressed concern about her daughter's constant need for reassurance and doubt in tasks, mirroring her own behaviors. Both exhibit patterns of checking, highlighting how children learn from parents. To disrupt this cycle, create memorable moments after completing tasks.

Secret No. 62

If you tend to doubt your actions right after completing them and have passed this habit on to your children, it's important not to blame them for exhibiting the same behavior. Instead, start associating those actions with specific 'remarkable' events. This practice will gradually resolve the issue on its own.

63

DON'T READ THIS CHAPTER

I'm sure that once you read the title of this chapter, you'll feel excited and eager to discover what's inside and why you shouldn't read it. What makes this chapter different? Do you feel curious? I'm sure you do because the human mind works that way. One of the most fascinating facts I've learned in my NLP (Neuro-Linguistic Programming) courses is that the mind can't process negative commands. Even when I guide people into a deep trance to help them make changes, I never say, "Don't think of anything else," because they inevitably will!

How many times a day do your children have to listen to 'Don't watch TV; don't waste time; don't fight with your brother; don't forget anything in the exam?' In reality, what happens is that, as you say 'don't', the mind wants to do it!

Let me describe a common scene:

Mom: 'Son, don't make a mess of the table while eating.'

Son: 'Yes, Mom!'

Son finishes eating, and the table is all messed up.

Mom: 'I told you not to make a mess because I knew you would. But you still didn't listen to me!'

As a parent, you think that because you know your children extremely well, you can predict what will happen. But in reality, in the above scenario, the child was given the choice to make a mess as a negative command. Hence, he did just that.

Here are some alternatives to negative commands.

What you must not say :

- Don't waste your time watching TV
- Don't forget anything in the exam.
- I know you are going to make a mess of the dining table
- Don't waste food
- You shouldn't fight with your brother/sister.

What you must say:

- Use your time wisely
- Eat everything that you have on your plate.
- Remember everything in the exam.
- Keep the dining table clean while eating.
- I know you will be friendly with your brother/sister.

SUMMARY OF CHAPTER 63/ IX

The chapter discusses how negative commands fail because the mind cannot process them. Examples illustrate how saying "don't" leads to unintended actions. Instead, using positive alternatives encourages desired behavior, such as "use your time wisely" or "keep the dining table clean," promoting better responses from children.

Secret No. 63

Positive commands make a huge difference to your children's behavior. Negative commands make them sub-consciously think they should do what they shouldn't! It has nothing to do with your children and everything to do with the words you use! Make a conscious change in your vocabulary—weed out the negatives!

64

BELIEFS ABOUT PARENTING

What do you think parenting is all about? Because what you believe is going to decide how you will feel about parenting and how you will handle the challenges of parenting. After all, it's all in the mind!

One cannot distinguish between True or False beliefs, only between Useful or Not-so-useful ones! If your beliefs about parenting are helpful, keep them. If they are not useful, question them. Check why you decided to think that way. Research goes on to show that your beliefs about parenting are a result of how you were parented.

Let's list some of the most useful parenting ideas. If you feel the same way, great; otherwise, decide to adopt them from now on!

1. Bringing up children is fun.
2. I am so fortunate to be a parent and to have children. Not every couple is gifted with children.
3. Being a parent helps me grow internally every day.
4. Parenting challenges make me emotionally stronger and give me lots of inner strength.

5. As a parent, I now occupy an important position in society. Society regards me as a more responsible individual.
6. Parenting is an excellent opportunity to shape an individual's life.
7. Parenting teaches me discipline, commitment, and sacrifice.
8. Parenting improves my communication skills and teaches me the need to be flexible.
9. Children create a special bond between one and my spouse.
10. Managing children and making them understand our views is easy.
11. I have such a great reason to return home from work — seeing my children's faces totally rejuvenates me!

Let us list some 'Myths' and 'Realities' about parenting. If you believe in any of these 'Myths,' get rid of them today!

Myth	**Reality**
1. Parenting is a pain and very stressful.	If you don't know how to be a great morn or dad, then it is a pain. As you decided to he a parent, So you should stand by it and enjoy it. Always feel the joy of parenting! If you don't have a child, it is even more painful — think of couples who are longing to have children.

2. Understanding children is very difficult. (Or) No parents can under-stand their children.	Your child is thinking the other may round — understanding parents is very difficult. If you are not able to understand anything, it does not mean that the thing is difficult. It only means, you have to put more efforts to learn.
3. Children often get distracted. It is very difficult to make them concentrate.	Children get distracted if what they are learning is not interesting enough! Once it becomes interesting, they can concentrate easily.
4. Teens are stubborn and don't like their parents.	Teens turn stubborn, as a result of stubborn parents. Teens, in fact, like people who listen to their views and new ideas. If parents can do that, they love their parents.
5. If one of the parents cannot spend a lot of time with the child, the child misses out a lot in life!	Not really. In fact, children do under-stand the challenges of real life. That makes them more adaptable and stronger.

6. My child has a lot to study and I really pity my child.	Nothing is 'a lot' for your child. It is just the way you see. The natural capabilities of a human being to learn is incredible and in any case we use very little of our total learning potential in the course of our life.
7. Siblings often fight with each other.	No. It depends on the kind of thoughts they are made to cultivate while still young. There are many siblings who understand, support and love each other a lot.
8. In today's world the competition is so high, it is difficult for my child to be successful.	In fact, in today's world, opportunities are plenty. Anyone who has the right mindset will make a mark. The number of individuals who are living theft dreams is very high.
9. Children are very easily influenced by society.	The reality is that children are more influenced by their parents than by society. Right from the moment of birth, your thoughts and actions influence them a lot.

10. Parents must not fight in front of children.	You must not fight in a manner that degrades the self-respect of your spouse. Differences of opinion can be discussed in front of your children, so that they learn more about reality and get the right perspectives on marriage.

SUMMARY OF CHAPTER 64/ IX

Parenting is shaped by beliefs and perspectives, which impact how challenges are handled. Useful beliefs enhance the parenting experience, while unhelpful ones should be questioned. Key useful ideas include viewing parenting as enjoyable, recognizing the privilege of having children, and acknowledging personal growth through parenting. Myths about parenting can hinder enjoyment; for instance, parenting is not inherently stressful, and understanding children requires effort. Distractions are due to unengaging material, teens desire understanding, and time spent apart can foster adaptability. Sibling dynamics depend on upbringing, while opportunities abound in today's competitive world. Lastly, children are more influenced by their parents than society, and healthy disagreements can offer valuable lessons.

Secret No. 64

Consciously cultivate those beliefs about parenthood which will enable you to become a better, happier and more positive parent.

CHAPTER X

ENCOURAGING CURIOSITY AND LEARNING

"Encouraging Curiosity and Learning," is dedicated to a child's natural inquisitiveness and transforming it into a lifelong passion for discovery, critical thinking, and personal growth. This chapter provides practical methods for parents and educators to create an environment where curiosity flourishes and learning becomes an engaging, joyful journey.

Curiosity is the engine of lifelong learning. By enhancing an environment that values questions, exploration, and real-world skills, parents and educators can help children develop into confident, adaptable, and enthusiastic learners ready to get in an ever changing world

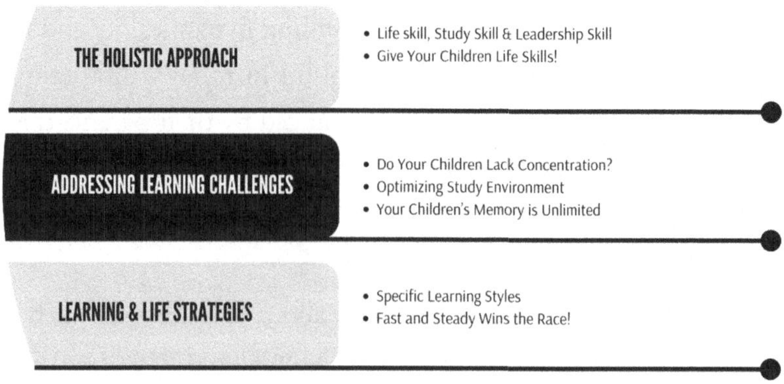

65

DO YOU WANT YOUR CHILDREN TO BE LIKE THE BOATMAN OR THE PROFESSOR?

Years ago, when we started our programmes for children, my team and I used to help children acquire skills in the following areas:

- Speed reading
- Memory
- Making effective notes
- Studying effectively
- Revision
- Taking examinations

Is mastering these skills important for a child to do well academically? I'm convinced that the answer is YES!

Are these skills enough to make children do well in life? Say a student is brilliant academically, does that guarantee that the child would go on to do well in life? You know as well as I do that the answer to that question is NO!

Excelling in academics and enjoying complete success in life do not always go together. However, they're both extremely important, the latter perhaps more so.

As a parent, do you want your children to do well in both areas - Study skills and Life skills?

Let me tell you a story

The Boatman and the Professor

Once upon a time, a professor had to cross a river. He went to a boatman and said to him, 'Can you take me across the river in your boat?'

The boatman replied, 'Yes professor, please sit down.' As soon as the professor was seated, he began to row.

On the way, the professor leant over the side of the boat to pick up a leaf that was floating on the water. Looking at the leaf he asked the boatman, 'Boatman, do you know what Botany is?'

The boatman responded, 'Botany? No, I don't know what that is.' The professor looked at him and said, 'You don't know what Botany is – a quarter of your life is gone!'

The boatman felt a little sad but continued to row. After a while, the professor picked up a stone from the river bed and asked the boatman, 'Boatman do you know what Geology is?' The boatman said, 'Geology? I've no idea what Geology means!'

The professor looked at him and said, 'You don't even know what Geology half of your life is gone!'

Now the boatman felt very sad, but he carried on rowing. Then, the boat hit a rock and water started to enter the boat. The boatman looked at the professor in the eye and asked him, 'Professor, do you know what swimming is?'

The professor replied, 'Swimming? I don't know what that is!'

The boatman smiled at the professor saying, 'You don't know what swimming is - your whole life is gone, for our boat is sinking!

I've told this story to thousands of parents in my seminars and asked them, 'Do you want your children to be like the boatman or the professor?' Do you know what answer they always give? BOTH! Why is that?

Doing well in life isn't about either study skills or life skills, but requires both. One of the most powerful secrets I have learnt is that children who have acquired both good study skills and life skills are the ones who go on to script success stories.

Your children are unique individuals, who should not be compared to or measured against others. Every child is special. Enable him or her to fulfil their dreams by providing them with the right tools.

Your role as a parent is that of a facilitator to help your children discover their true potential. It is, therefore, important for you to help your children develop not only study skills to deal with the academic and professional challenges of today's world but also life skills to deal with the practical problems that life poses.mic and professional challenges and life skills to handle the practicalities life throws their way.

SUMMARY OF CHAPTER 65/ X

When we launched programs for children, we emphasized essential skills like speed reading, memory enhancement, effective note-taking, and exam preparation to support academic success. However, excelling academically does not ensure success in life. Life skills often hold greater significance. The story of the Boatman and the Professor illustrates that knowledge alone isn't enough; practical skills are vital. Parents should strive to help children cultivate both study and life skills, guiding them to achieve their unique potential without comparison, as balanced development leads to future success.

Secret No. 65

Holistic Development: Nurturing both academic abilities and life skills in your child will ensure they become adaptable and successful adults.

66

GIVE YOUR CHILDREN LIFE SKILLS!

One of the many ironies about parenting is that although every parent knows that education and degrees alone can't create a promising future for their children, most parents are still only concerned about their children's studies. Studies are important. And I am sure that as a parent you spend much of your time and money imparting knowledge to your children about science, history, geography, maths, computers, commerce, economics, foreign languages and so on.

But have you ever tried to help your children acquire any of the following:

- Time Management skills,
- High self-esteem,
- Self-motivation strategies,
- Empowering notions,
- Leadership skills,
- Healthy living strategies?

After all these life skills prove critical in the long run. How will your children develop a well-rounded personality, without these?

Certain schools make these 'life skills' a part of the curriculum, but most of the time it is given the least preference in the academic arena. It isn't included in exam syllabi and children are not graded upon it! And, therefore, invariably both parents and children don't give much importance to these subtle but crucial aspects of education.

Some school activities indirectly impart a few of these skills to children. Unfortunately, the children who come forward and avail these opportunities are usually the ones who are already good in these areas. These qualities come in handy from an early age, for instance:

- To be able to act in a school play, the child should already be good at public speaking and dramatics, and not be timid or stage-shy.
- To compare an event on stage, the child must be free of inhibitions.
- To participate in a dance competition, the child must have a healthy mix of confidence and the right skills.

Usually, the children who don't exhibit these skills at the first instant, miss out on the game altogether. So, as a parent, you must let your children learn more about life and living, than what their school books teach, How do you ensure that?

1. Introduce your children to the world of books. Through stories, real or fictional, they will learn many positive, life-affirming things, and will learn to garner sustenance for the

soul. They will also have a wider perspective of life and will learn that there is more to life than academics.

2. Watch positive, inspirational films with your children.
3. Engage your children in various activities - both outdoors and indoors. Let them play in the sun with the children of the neighbourhood - that way, they will learn how to get along with people, and the importance of team spirit. Let them learn some sport or the other so that their health and mind are in perfect order. Let them help you around the house so that they know a thing or two about the running of households too.
4. Only sending them to various classes (singing, swimming, tennis, etc.) won't do. Pass on *your experiences* about life to your children. Spend time with them talking about these things!

SUMMARY OF CHAPTER 66/ X

While parents often prioritize academic achievement, essential life skills like time management, self-esteem, and leadership are vital for long-term success. Many schools focus on traditional subjects, neglecting these skills, which can hinder well-rounded development. Parents should introduce relevant books, watch inspirational films, encourage outdoor play, involve children in sports, and share personal experiences to foster a broader understanding of life.

Secret No. 66

Academic education is just one part of your child's overall development. It's essential to help your child develop crucial 'life skills' as well!

67

DO YOUR CHILDREN LACK CONCENTRATION?

When we hold training camps for children, we talk to parents about the challenges and difficulties their children experience in studies and behavior. The most prevalent issue for both parents and kids is difficulty concentrating. Parents often say things like:

- "Whenever my child picks up a science book, he soon says, 'I feel hungry. Should I eat before I continue reading?"
- "It seems like my kids only think about fixing household items, like changing a remote battery, as soon as study time begins."
- "My child can't sit still to study for more than a few minutes."
- "Every day, they have a new excuse to get distracted from their studies. I don't know how to help them focus!"

But what is the underlying issue? I ask parents: Is it that your children can't concentrate at all? How long do they stay focused when playing computer games? Parents often respond, "Oh, they can keep playing those games indefinitely!" So, why do they stay focused on games but not studying? Where do their interest and concentration come from when they're gaming?

When you think about it, mobile games captivate children because they engage the whole brain. They activate both the left and right brain functions. How do they use the left brain during gaming? Online games have levels requiring players to meet certain criteria involving calculations and strategic thinking. They know exactly how many points they need from each action and how many total points they want by the game's end. Even adults might take time to calculate this, but children do it instantly, an exercise of logic, sequencing, and math, which are left-brain functions.

How is the right brain involved? Mobile games are colorful and have rhythmic background music. They require creativity and imagination. Children might create characters, name them, and assign them different cars, all activities that require creativity. Imagination, music, rhythm, and color perception are right brain functions.

The most effective learning method engages both sides of the brain at once. For any student, whether left-brain or right-brain dominant, simultaneous use of both brain sides facilitates focus and concentration.

There are no truly inattentive students, only inadequate teaching methods that fail to capture their attention. Consider creative pedagogical approaches to make learners happy and engaged. Let study time transform into fun time!

SUMMARY OF CHAPTER 66/ X

Training camps reveal that children struggle with concentration while studying, often distracted by various thoughts. Parents notice their children can focus intensely on video games, indicating that these games engage both brain hemispheres. To improve focus in studies, teaching methods should also engage both sides of the brain, turning learning into an enjoyable experience.

Secret No. 67

To ignite your child's enthusiasm and concentration, create study sessions that activate both sides of the brain, just like their favorite computer games! Blend logical challenges with creative tasks, using vibrant colors and rhythmic sounds to make learning an exciting adventure. This balanced approach turns study time into an engaging and joyful experience that they'll look forward to!

68

THE STUDY ENVIRONMENT

Parents often ask me to throw some light upon the kind of environment their children should have while preparing for their exams. An ideal environment is the one that will enable your children to concentrate on their studies.

It always helps to have a fixed place for study. This should be a place with minimum distracting elements. If children have a place where they are used to studying, then that becomes their appropriate behavior in that environment. Whenever they sit there, they'll feel ready to work. It's not a good idea to study with their mobile phone next to them.

A common challenge faced by children is when they want to take a short break and decide to watch reels for just five minutes. But the time flies. Five minutes becomes a few hours. Why? Watching mobile content is addictive. One of the common challenges that people face these days is how to keep their children focused during study holidays and before exams!

Instead, for taking a break, it's better to choose activities like walking, listening to inspirational audio, playing indoor games like carom, or exercising. However, taking regular breaks is essential. The best way is to take a ten-minute break when a particular task is completed, or one in every two hours.

Parents must understand that not everyone needs to study in a quiet environment. Some children find it easier to study when there's music playing in the background. A reasonably fast tempo helps certain children to stay focused. In fact, fast music helps to cut down other thoughts that run in the mind.

Certain specific kinds musk like Classical and Instrumental music have been shown to help in the learning process. It is important, however, to avoid songs with lyrics since it invariably distracts!

Adequate light is important to prevent straining the eye. The temperature of a room can also affects the concentration of students. If facilities permit, I recommend 20 degrees centigrade or a slightly lower temperature for learning. It keeps the mind alert. Dressing in layers makes it easier for children to control their temperature.

If it's warm, it's easy to fall asleep. Too cold, and it's hard to concentrate. Studying in bed is a definite no. People behave in certain ways according to their environment. Once children lie on their beds, their bodies tell them it's time to go to sleep, and they'll find it almost impossible to stay awake.

SUMMARY OF CHAPTER 68/ X

An ideal study environment for children should minimize distractions and promote concentration. Establishing a fixed study space helps reinforce appropriate study behavior. Avoid mobile phones. Instead of passive breaks like using mobile phones, encourage active ones like walking or playing indoor games. Suitable lighting and a comfortable room temperature around 20 degrees Celsius enhance focus. Music can aid concentration, but avoid lyrical songs, and discourage studying in bed to prevent sleepiness.

Secret No. 68

Help your children create the right environment for productive hours of studying.

69

YOUR CHILDREN'S MEMORY IS UNLIMITED

Do you think that your children have poor memories? Are your children finding it very difficult to recall things? Do you want to test your children's memory power? Take a look at the list of words below. Ask your children to memorize them in such a way that when you say a word from the set 1, they can recall the corresponding word from set 2.

Set 1	**Set 2**
Chair	Tree
Pencil	Bulb
Airplane	Train
Phone	Book
Pen	Shirt
Ball	Suitcase
Pin	Cinema
Projector	Lion
Bag	Mirror

Let your children read the list for a while, and then ask them what they can remember. Do your children find this difficult? Let me offer you a strategy to make it easier. Ask your children to link or associate the first word with the second word in a funny or outstanding way.

Say for example, the first word 'chair' must be linked to the second word 'tree' in a fun way. Let's imagine that a lot of chairs are hanging from a tree instead of fruit. See the tree full of hanging chairs in your mind's eye.

Go to the next set Pencil and bulb. How can you associate them? ' Imagine a huge red pencil with its bulb at the end flashing from it. So then , when I say 'pencil', what comes to the mind? Bulb. When I say tree? Chairs. Is this becoming caster or not?

Now, link 'book' with 'bag.' Imagine a huge bag overflowing with books. Ask your children to complete the rest of the mink and see the magic for yourself.

Now what do you think of your children's memory? Is it the power of memory, or of the strategy used by your children? Every human being in this world is born with 1 million million neurons in their brain. Neurons are the cells found in the brain, and each neuron has more memory capacity than the most powerful computer ever invented. So, stop telling your children that their memory is bad or poor. If they hear that enough times, they'll start believing that it's true.

It saddens me that the market is flooded by products that supposedly improve memory, and that parents also get carried away by the advertisements about the products and start feeding them to their children. Once children start taking these things, they lose their faith in the power of their natural memory and start believing that the quality of their memory is only due to these tablets!

By using the tight strategies, children can learn various ways to recall things faster. You can help them by implanting in them the belief that they are capable of remembering anything!

SUMMARY OF CHAPTER 69/ X

If you believe your children struggle with memory, try testing it using two word sets. Have them memorize words from Set 1 and match them with Set 2. Encourage them to create funny associations for easier recall, like imagining chairs hanging from a tree. Highlight that memory can improve with strategies, not products. Reinforce their natural memory capacity and remove doubts about their abilities, enabling confidence in their recall skills.

Secret No. 69

Help your children implement the right strategies to improve their memory. It will make a world of difference to their confidence levels.

70

WHAT DO YOU TEACH THEM ABOUT THE RICH AND FAMOUS?

I've often asked people, ' What do you feel about the rich and the famous?

Some of their responses are based on highly stereotypical motions, which they unconsciously tend to pass on to their children.

Make sure, you share with your children the success stories of entrepreneurs who started from scratch and now find themselves amongst the richest people of the world. People like Sabeer Bhatia, Richard Branson, Ray Kroc - The founder of McDonalds, Sam Walton -the founder of Walmart, Michael Dell - the founder of Dell Computer Corporation, Anita Riddick the founder of a chain of environmentally -friendly cosmetics stores and the like.

These are people who learnt to follow their heart and believe in their dreams. Through their hard work, creativity and dedication they achieved what they set out to do. Don't let the wrong mentality be a hindrance in fulfilling your children's dreams.

If you want your children to be wealthy or famous, you can't pass on wrong notions about wealth to them. Being rich and famous is a mindset. If you want your children to be rich, your children must learn to respect and learn from the examples . of those who are rich. They should be driven by their dreams and ambitions.

Often people believe that for earning a fortune, we need to sacrifice our morals and ethics or sometimes even use illegal methods. We tend to pass these notions to our little ones, making them skeptical about the lifestyles of the rich and the famous. You should share with your children success stories of these individuals rather than making your children doubt their ethics. Make sure these stories work as an inspiration. Also share with your children their benevolent actions.

Warren Buffett intends to give away nearly all his wealth to philanthropy, having pledged in 2006 to donate most of his fortune. He recently updated his will to allocate 99.5% of his remaining wealth to a charitable trust managed by his children after his death, emphasizing his lifelong commitment to charitable giving.

SUMMARY OF CHAPTER 70/ X

Responses regarding the rich often reflect stereotypes that can be passed to children. Share success stories of entrepreneurs, encouraging a positive mindset about wealth and fame, while highlighting charitable actions of successful individuals.

Secret No. 70

Teach your children the right perspectives about wealth; it can be achieved through legal, moral, and ethical means.

71

FAST AND STEADY WINS THE RACE!

I watched a video, which showed the famous story of the hare and the tortoise: The hare and a tortoise go in for a race. The hare, very proud of its speed, starts running and, after a while, when it has gone much ahead, decides to rest under the shadow of a tree and dozes off to sleep. As a slow walker, the tortoise reaches the point where the hare is sleeping, crosses it without waking up the hare, and readies the finish line. Then the hare wakes up only to realize the fact that it has lost the race!

The moral was flashed on the screen, 'Slow and steady wins the race.' In these fast-changing times, we must question the basis of all the teachings we impart to our children. 'The slow and steady' may or may not win the race. It wholly depends on the circumstances. Even though being steadfast is a virtue that will help a child win a race, being slow may not. Therefore, your aim as parents should be to make your children understand that they need to find their own pace rather than burn out in the rat race.

Therefore, parents should teach their children to judge a situation, determine the best possible option, and consider the consequences before they decide on a course of action. When you're teaching your children similar stories, ask yourself the following questions:

1. Is it really going to be beneficial for my children?
2. Are the story's morals relevant to the times we live in?

Be prepared with examples to support your teachings. Encourage your children to see things from several different perspectives so that they develop a broader view of life and think objectively.

Choose books and Videos that let your children express forthright thoughts and beliefs instead of touching just any book or video.

SUMMARY OF CHAPTER 71/ X

Hope you are aware of the story: The hare, overconfident, falls asleep, allowing the tortoise to win in a race. The moral, "Slow and steady wins the race," prompts reflection on teaching values. Parents should help children discern situations, adapt to change, and think critically, fostering broader perspectives and individual insights for life.

Secret No. 71

Fast and steady runners are more likely to win the race. Teach your children the practical and the probable. Fast and Steady Wins the Race!

CHAPTER XI

FINANCIAL LITERACY AND RESPONSIBILITY

"Financial Literacy and Responsibility," empowers children to develop essential money management skills, a healthy attitude toward wealth, and a sense of social responsibility. This chapter blends practical activities, mindset development, and life lessons to prepare children for financial independence and generosity.

Financial literacy is a life skill that should be nurtured from an early age. By combining practical money management, a positive mindset, and the value of giving, parents and educators can equip children to make wise financial choices, pursue ambitious goals, and contribute meaningfully to society

MINDSET & GOALS

- The Habit of Saving: Create Your Children's Piggy Banks
- The Mindset of a Millionaire
- Should You Only Dream 'Realistic'?

GIVING & PHILANTHROPY

- Teaching Children the Power of Giving
- Do You Donate Blood?

PARENTING & LIFE LESSONS

- Children's Perspectives on Life
- Common Parental Questions & Answers

72

DO YOU DONATE BLOOD?

I was writing this immediately after donating blood alongside hundreds who participated in our adults training program and the parents of children training program. It fills me with a profound sense of fulfillment and makes life seem more meaningful. The experience these parents and children leave with is truly incredible. Children are curious and ask their parents many questions about donating blood, such as "Why should we donate blood?" "What happens with the blood we give?" "Who benefits from it?" "Will the blood come back?" The answers they receive can change their perspective in significant ways.

By donating blood, you become a positive role model for your children, teaching some of life's most valuable lessons When asked, "Why should I donate blood?" the child gets to receive one of these responses:

- It adds meaning to life.
- It saves the lives of people I might never meet.
- It helps me feel connected to my community.
- Giving blood is one of the most precious gifts.

The concepts that your child will grasp when they see you donate blood are inspiring. They will gradually develop the most powerful attitude - loving people without expecting anything in return. This shows them the magical power of human connection.

Donate blood today!

SUMMARY OF CHAPTER 72/ XI

Donating blood fosters fulfillment and meaningful connections. Children learn valuable life lessons about altruism and community from witnessing this act, shaping their perspectives and promoting empathy. Donate blood today.

Secret No. 72

Every well-rounded individual has learned to give selflessly for the betterment of others. Their heart naturally reaches out to those in need. The best time to instill this mindset in your children is when they are young. Give them the chance to understand the rewards of donating blood and inspire them to become caring individuals. Demonstrate through your actions, like like donating blood, how to contribute meaningfully to humanity.

73

SHOULD YOU ONLY DREAM 'REALISTIC'?

What happened to your childhood dreams? When you were young, what did you think was possible in your life? I came across a study that explained that when people are young, they see themselves as "superhumans," capable of achieving a lot in their lives.

- You never see yourself as a spectator but as the match's hero.
- You don't see yourself as a person working for somebody else but as a boss running a multimillion-dollar business.
- You never see yourself as merely reading a book but writing a great book yourself.
- You never see yourself as a patient but as a doctor.
- You never see yourself as a passenger but as a pilot.
- You don't see yourself as a citizen but as someone who can influence the government.

What happens to these dreams? What happens to these possibilities? When I mentor children, guiding them to set goals for their lives, it's an incredible experience. Almost every one of them believes they can be outstanding. Becoming the world's best scientist, the top cardiologist, a pilot, an Olympic gold medalist, a Nobel Prize winner, an astronaut, the best dancer, or the fastest person on Earth are some of their dreams.

The Positivity Hub experience help children consciously resist the "be realistic" way of thinking, which can often make them give up on their dreams. Whenever children set high goals, they invariably face a lot of put-downs from the world around them.

Often, this comes from their parents because their parents love them and never want them to fail. Parents feel that some things may be achieved only by special people and don't want to risk their children failing. Their protectiveness, a wish to shield their child from the pain of failure, makes them say, "Be realistic."

What may be realistic for you is not realistic for your children. Nothing in this world seems realistic until someone achieves it!

When I was twenty-six and decided to choose my current career path, it wasn't realistic at all, and many people advised me against it. However, the techniques and experience I'd gained from world-class training allowed me to hone my skills and understand how it was up to me to make it possible.

SUMMARY OF CHAPTER 73/ XI

Childhood dreams often view life in limitless possibilities. Young individuals see themselves as heroes, business leaders, authors, doctors, pilots, and influencers. However, societal pressures and protective parental instincts may stifle these aspirations, urging "realism." Mentoring children helps them resist this mindset, encouraging them to pursue extraordinary goals, proving that achievement begins with believing in the impossible.

Secret No. 73

Your children have it in them to make the impossible. Possible! So, don't be 'realistic' and decide on their behalf what is achievable and what is not!

74

THE HABIT OF SAVING: CREATE YOUR CHILDREN'S PIGGY BANKS

Do you ever discuss finance with your children? If not, start now. Teaching your children early in life the need to plan and invest will help them later manage their finances better! Teach your children the habit of saving. I've seen several parents who feel that money is not a fit subject of discussion for a child.

I've asked parents, ' If money isn't a subject fit for your child, why do you want them to study well? The response is usually that the parent wants them to be successful. What do you mean by successful? Does success mean getting a good job or doing a good business? Don't you also want them to earn a lot of money? " They always say. Definitely, lots of money! " If you want them to carry a lot of money, you have to teach them how to save and invest. I have seen lots of people who aren't rich yet, not because they don't carry a lot, but because they don't save a lot.

An amazing miracle, ' Edison says, is the power of compounding, Which multiplies money to a huge size in a longer period of time. Start the habit of saving for your children as soon as possible. Not tomorrow, but today. If they don't have a piggy bank, buy them one today. Open a bank account in your children's name. Let your children feel a sense of belonging. Arrange specific times, at least once a month, to visit the bank. Teach your children about things such as savings accounts, fixed deposits, Investments, unit trusts, and bonds. Cheques, cash, and credit cards are things that schools are unlikely to teach them. Start teaching them how the bank works. Remember, you're creating a huge impact in their life. Many of us learned these things when we had to. Why should your children wait?

SUMMARY OF CHAPTER 74/ XI

Discussing finance with children is vital. Teach them to save and invest early to manage finances better. They need to understand money for success. Empower them with knowledge about savings accounts, investments, and bank operations. Start today; the earlier they learn, the greater their financial future will be.

Secret No. 74

What makes the difference in life is not how much you earn; it is how much you save.

Teach your child to save and lead by example.

75

THE MINDSET OF A MILLIONAIRE

When you want your children to live a life of prosperity, you shouldn't just save money but rather create the mindset of a millionaire. The mindset of a millionaire is very different from that of others. Millionaires view wealth and money differently. They are millionaires first in their minds and then in the real world.

You need to train your children's minds not to focus on financial survival but on financial abundance. There is a huge difference between the two!

Survival is making enough money to pay off your monthly bills, ensuring that the family and self have enough to survive. Survival is the mindset of scarcity. Survivors think, 'Is there enough money in this world for me to make?'

Abundance is the mindset of millionaires. They feel that the universe is filled with a fortune and that however much you take, it can never be reduced. The total wealth in the universe is only increasing, and that is the reason we see more millionaires today than a decade or two before! People are becoming millionaires at a younger age today. Share with your children the stories of

Google, Apple, Reliance and Nvidia, and give real-life examples like Warren Buffet, Elon Musk, and Bill Gates, of individuals who became amazingly wealthy at a very young age. Creating wealth is easier than ever today.

The rich invest money. When they invest money, they know there is a timeframe to be repaid and that the returns are huge. Building an investment and being in a job are different. When you are at a job, by the end of every month, you are paid for your efforts. Millionaires may start small, but they have big dreams. They focus on the big dream, and that is what keeps them growing.

It is human nature for children to have big dreams, and your job is to nurture them. You need to make them believe that being a millionaire or being a middle class is a matter of choice. They have

the choice, and the efforts required are the same. The only difference is that of the mindset.

If your children ask you how rich they can be, tell them they can be as rich as they want.

If they have the right mindset, your children can become millionaires too. Impress your child with the idea of abundance. There is enough for everyone to be rich. The world can be a place made up of millionaires. There are enough riches in the world to make each and everyone a millionaire!

SUMMARY OF CHAPTER 75/ XI

To cultivate a prosperous life for your children, instill a millionaire's mindset rather than simply saving money. Emphasize financial abundance over survival. Millionaires view wealth as limitless, believing in ample opportunities. Share success stories and demonstrate that wealth creation is attainable. Encourage big dreams, reinforcing that becoming a millionaire is a choice influenced by mindset. Abundance is possible; there are enough resources for everyone to thrive.

Secret No. 75

Being a millionaire is about the mindset. If you make a millionaire bankrupt, he will become a millionaire again!

76

TEACH YOUR CHILDREN THE POWER OF GIVING

Will you be happy if your children become achievers? Is it enough if they are first-rankers at school and in extracurricular activities? Is there something else to their lives?

What is the purpose of our existence? Teach your children the power of giving. What can give to fulfillment is not success and money but the joy of giving. The purpose of life is created through the service we do for people around us. No matter how high a position you reach in your job or how much money you make, ultimately, what matters the most is your contribution to society.

A boy went to an ice cream parlor to order an ice cream. So he called the waitress and asked her to bring the menu. As she brought the card, he went through the list of ice creams and started enquiring about the prices of all the different varieties available. As she told him the names and prices, he counted his money, mostly coins. He repeatedly rechecked the prices, and the waitress became irritated. Indeed, he took a long time to decide. The waitress lost her patience because it had been a long day for her. So, she asked him rudely, Are you going to order now?' while muttering to herself.

Then, the little boy ordered the cheapest possible ice cream, which helped him save a few coins. The waitress served him quite unwillingly. After a while, the boy left, and the waitress went to clean the table. There, she found a few coins left as a tip. Surprisingly, she also found a thank you note saying, 'Thanks for your service! This little money is all I can afford to give you.'

The waitress was really touched. Her eyes became wet. She realized that the boy was actually spending time going through the menu list to find the cheapest possible combination because, in the end, he wanted to leave some money as a tip. Like this exemplary little boy, let giving come naturally to your child!

SUMMARY OF CHAPTER 76/ XI

Happiness for children lies beyond achievements; it encompasses the joy of giving. Life's purpose is found in serving others, not just in success or wealth. A boy, choosing the cheapest ice cream to leave a tip, exemplifies this lesson, highlighting the importance of kindness and generosity in one's life.

Secret No. 76

Teach your children how to share and how to give. Remember, this lesson is more important than teaching them how to acquire!

77

ELEVEN THINGS YOUR CHILDREN WANT TO SAY ABOUT LIFE AND WHAT YOU CAN LEARN FROM THEM

These are your children's views based on what they see:

1. You told me to take responsibility, but recently, I saw you blaming your boss and office fast turning up for my school function. Remember, you are my role model.
2. When I choose an expensive dress, you can be frank with me about our budget or the constraints you may face in paying for it. I can understand family constraints. Please help me understand these things better. Never buy me whatever I want!
3. You needn't feel bad about pointing out my mistakes; you need to correct me.
4. I could see tears of happiness in Granddad's eyes when you gave him the watch he loved. Thanks for those kind of wonderful gestures of love that you express to your parents! I will do the same for you.

5. You can fight in front of me, Mom and Dad! Let me also understand that marriage is sometimes about misunderstandings, but it's always about the special connection of love and affection!
6. I am sorry I lied to you about clearing the rubbish, but do you remember the other day you told me you were visiting your friend, but the same friend called here while you were away?! I learn from you!
7. You always tell me that I must be a responsible citizen, but the other day, when we were driving together, you ignored traffic signals and road rules. What you do affects me more than what you say!
8. You want me to pursue medicine because that was your dream, but please understand that I have a dream of my own.
9. If you want me to be more responsible, you must allow me to make some important decisions.
10. You promised to take me to the fun park, but you were totally tied up in the office that day. This makes me think it is sometimes okay to make false promises to please someone.
11. You took me to the orphanage the other day, and when I saw the children there, I understood how lucky I am to have loving parents. Do these acts of kindness to others, and I will realize I am gifted!

SUMMARY OF CHAPTER 77/ XI

Children observe their parents' behaviors closely. They note instances of hypocrisy, like blame-shifting and broken promises.

They appreciate honesty about finances and lessons about love, mistakes, and responsibility. They seek understanding of their own aspirations, witness kindness towards others, and recognize the importance of genuine connections over superficial gestures. They value consistency between words and actions.

Secret No. 77

Communication is not the only integral part of a child-parent relationship; you should also set an example for them while helping them find their own identities.

78

ELEVEN OF THE MOST POPULAR QUESTIONS PARENTS HAVE ASKED ME: MY ANSWERS AND WHAT YOU CAN LEARN FROM

1. *Why do my children lack concentration?*
   Is that always the case? I am sure it isn't. When their study methods aren't interesting, they get diverted very quickly! A lack of concentration is nothing but a lack of interest, which is caused because they don't employ the right ways of learning.
2. *Can children understand these concepts When you say goals, beliefs, etc.?*
   Think about people who started achieving from a young age, like Sachin Tendulkar, Bill Gates, and Cristiano Ronaldo. What did they have in common? They were sure of what they wanted (goals); they had empowering beliefs ('I can do it', 'I can be the best in the world'). What each child needs is a trigger!

3. *Can I give my children tablets to enhance their memory?*
   That's the worst thing you can do as a parent. Your children's memory is incredibly powerful! There are about 1 million million neurons, and every neuron is more powerful than the most powerful computer ever invented. If your children can't remember something, it only means that they have not used the proper methods to store and recall the information.
4. *My child is average. How can you help?*
   First, stop telling them that. This is the biggest favor you can do for your children! Whenever you say, 'My children are average,' you are making the children average in studies and life. When your children see themselves as average, they will expect only average lives, too. On the contrary, teach your children to surpass themselves and dream big! Never imprison them in your definition of averageness.
5. *My children's eating habits are very bad.* They never bother about the timing and are only keen to eat junk food. What can I do?
   Make your children realize they are 'gifted' to get a plate of food daily. Not everyone in this world gets it. Your children must remember that some children struggle to get one meal a day and work very hard to get a meal. Soon enough, these problems will disappear.
6. *How come my child hates his brother or sister?*
   It's time for you to stop comparing them. It would help if you learned to look at what is unique and what you can appreciate in each child. Comparisons make children think you don't like them as they are. Being young leads them to the simple conclusion that you prefer the sibling—and this leads to animosity between them!

7. *Is it always difficult to manage teens?*
   If you start believing it, it is going to be very difficult. You need to ensure that you have a great relationship with your children. Studies always say that only those children who don't have great relationships at home tend to indulge in anti-social activities!
8. *Will changes happen fast?*
   Changes happen in a moment! Positive changes in your child's life can happen for only two reasons: self-realization or a disaster in life. Once your child realizes, 'I do things for myself,' 'I am gifted,' and 'I must make my life really meaningful,' then these positive changes happen in an instant!
9. *Can I scold my child?*
   You must! Scold them when you definitely know their behavior is not useful. If you never scold your child, they will never learn that what they have done is not helpful and will take you for granted.
10. *My child suffers from excessive sleeping. How can I stop it?*
    Excessive sleeping is just a symptom. It arises because of a lack of inspiring goals. Once they set inspiring goals, they find little time to sleep.
11. *How are you able to achieve massive positive changes in the minds of children in just four days?*
    We don't teach children; we create an experience of a lifetime that makes the children say to themselves, 'I MUST CHANGE!'

SUMMARY OF CHAPTER 78/ XI

Children often lack concentration due to unengaging study methods, leading to disinterest. Understanding concepts like goals and beliefs is crucial for motivation; successful individuals from a young age had clear aspirations and empowering beliefs. Tablets do not enhance memory; effective learning methods are necessary. Labeling a child as "average" can limit their potential, so encourage them to dream big instead. Teaching gratitude for food can improve poor eating habits, while avoiding comparisons among siblings fosters better relationships. Managing teens is easier with strong family bonds, and positive changes occur through self-realization or challenges. Scolding is necessary for behavior correction. Excessive sleeping often signals a lack of goals, while impactful experiences can inspire change in just four days.

Secret No. 78

Help your children develop the ***'I must change'*** attitude.

CHAPTER XII

PARENTING STYLES AND STRATEGIES

"Parenting Styles and Strategies," explores the diverse approaches parents use to guide, nurture, and support their children, the importance of flexibility, self-awareness, and ongoing learning in the parenting journey.

There is no single "right" way to parent. The most effective strategies combine warmth, structure, empathy, and adaptability. By staying attuned to your child's needs, modeling positive behaviors, and remaining open to learning and growth, you can enhance a healthy, resilient, and connected family

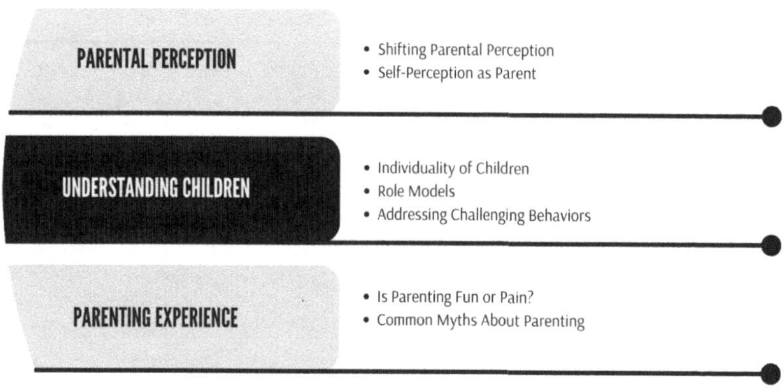

79

SEEING BEYOND THE SHELL: SHIFTING PARENTAL PERCEPTION

I am going to share with you one of my most recent experiences in family counselling about a fourteen-year-old boy. His parents told me gravely, 'Our son lives in a shell.'

I had a separate session with the child who came across as really open and forthcoming. He told me that he was the only son and loved his parents very much. I was a stranger to him and yet, we had a wonderful discussion for quite a while.

I purposely asked him some intensely emotional questions to see how well he could express his feelings, and I was touched to find out how much he loved his father. I understood soon enough that there was an error in perception on the part of the parents. If a child truly lives in a shell, it usually takes much more time for me to discover his true feelings. I realised that the 'existence of the shell' was his parents' perception and not exactly true.

The next twenty-five minutes that I spent with his parents were crucial. When I asked his parents to tell me what the problem was, they said, 'He lives in a shell. Both of them answered in the same words. They could offer numerous examples to support this idea. How he misses opportunities because he lives in a shell. How he never answers his teachers. How he always chooses to play with younger children. How, when at home, he never fights for anything, and even when scolded goes into his room, locks the door and stays there for a while. HE LIVES IN A SHELL!

Then I asked them this question. 'Tell me where his shell is now?' They looked at me diffidently and then looked at one another. I repeated my question more forcefully. 'Tell me where his shell is now?'

Then his mother started to speak. 'No, what I mean is…' Before she finished, I asked them again, 'Tell me where his shell is now?' She stopped and said, 'It's at home.'

'Is it? What does it look like? What colour is it?'

They hadn't expected that question. I pushed harder. 'What does it look like? What colour is it?' Finally, the answer came. 'It looks like a shell and it's BLACK'

'Have you seen it?'

'Yeah! He always gets into it!'

Now I know the way out! In his parents' minds, are stark images of their child in a shell, a tough, black shell! Once his parents began to see him in that way, whatever he did, whatever he said, they could not see or hear. Because to them he lived inside a BLACK shell!

For the next fifteen minutes, I worked with the parents attempting to break the image that they had built up over the last ten or eleven years. Gradually through the intense, emotionally challenging session, they could break that hard, black shell that they held in their mind.

They finally managed to release their child from the 'shell' in which they had imprisoned him in for the last fourteen years! It was an amazing moment for the couple. They cried in relief, hugged one another, felt deep regret about the past, and experienced great joy knowing that their son wouldn't be in the 'shell' any longer.

SUMMARY OF CHAPTER 79/ XII

A family's counseling revealed a fourteen-year-old boy's genuine expressiveness, contrasting his parents' belief he lived in a "shell." Through discussion, the parents recognized their misconceptions, ultimately feeling relief and joy as they freed their son from this restrictive perception.

Secret No. 79

Consider if you've unknowingly boxed your child in with your thoughts. Break down these limits to help them become who they truly are.

80

I AM JUST A MOM/DAD!

Who are you?

Does this sound like a silly question? Many women answer this with – 'I am just a mom.' What they mean is, 'I don't work anywhere and I am 'just' spending my time being a mother to my children.'

When a parent tells me that 'she is *just* a mom or I am just a dad', it only tells me that he or she does not see the greatness of this role and considers it a nominal identity. Though anybody can have a child, not everybody can be a Mom or Dad! In the words of **Virginia Satir**, author and one of the most outstanding family therapists, whose research studies have taught me a great deal.

I regard parenting as the hardest, most complicated, anxiety-ridden, sweat-and-blood-producing job in the world. Succeeding requires the ultimate in patience, common sense, commitment, humour, tact, love, wisdom, awareness, and knowledge. At the same time, it holds the possibility for the most rewarding, joyous experience of a lifetime, namely, that of being a successful guides to a new and unique human being.

Being 'just a Mom/Dad' is very different from being a super mom or super dad who has the ultimate potential for patience, a lot of common sense, deep commitment to giving the very best to children, a strong sense of humour, unconditional love, and a great deal of flexibility and wisdom to handle parenting challenges. Define right now what your identity is as a parent. What kind of mom or dad are you?

Inspiring?	Awesome?
Strict?	Cool?
Lousy?	Loving?
Nagging?	Understanding?
Fun Loving?	Critical?
Motivating?	Stressed Out?
Stubborn?	Dishonest?
Caring?	Over-Protective?
Responsible?	Supportive?
Learning?	Encouraging?
Joyous?	Terrific?

Choose your identity. You need to choose your identity as per the need, which means you need to be very flexible in shifting between identities. At certain times you need to be a strict parent, at other times, an inspiring parent or a fun-loving parent! You must learn how to avoid being a nagging parent or a 'lousy' parent. Define who you are!

SUMMARY OF CHAPTER 80/ XII

Many women say "I am just a mom," downplaying their role. Parenting demands exceptional patience, wisdom, and love. It's crucial to recognize the significance of being a parent. Choose your identity flexibly, adapting as needed between being strict, fun-loving, inspiring, or supportive to nurture your child's growth effectively.

Secret No. 80

Parents, it would help if you chose your identity depending on the need of the hour. So, be flexible in shifting between various positive parental identities.

81

WHAT'S TRUE FOR YOU MAY NOT BE TRUE FOR YOUR CHILDREN

What's true for you isn't always true for your children! What do I mean by this? You might be in the habit of saying things like the following:

- I was no good at drawing when I was in school.
- Sport isn't my area, it's the same for my child.
- We get tired easily (parent and child).
- If you don't have a hot drink, you'll get a headache.
- Talking onstage is very difficult.
- If you don't eat on time, you will fall sick.
- You won't remember anything if you read very fast.

'Remember, these are all your 'problems', for want of a better world. Unfortunately, many parents unconsciously assume that their children will face exactly the same kind of things that they did.

Children are very sensitive to their parents' words. If you are negative about your abilities and limitations, your children may copy you. If you assume that your limitations apply to your children, they'll believe you. You are setting your children up for failure. Often, they will take your word and won't even bother to 'try' out many things!

Remember, your children are individuals with different skills and abilities. Negative assumptions are useless when it comes to learning from the world. When you were young, your life was filled with possibilities. You felt that everything was possible! Your children too live in a world filled with possibilities of flying planes and becoming adventures!

Take a sheet of paper and write down all the dreams you had when you were very young. Look at how big they were, how exciting. What happened to those dreams? Later on as you grew up, you started learning about REALITY! The world started telling you, 'Be realistic, don't be greedy.'

If say, someone like Bill Clinton had accepted that sort of a 'be realistic' mindset, the USA might not have had him as the President. Clinton was born and brought up in a small American town. When he started school, he used to tell his teachers 'I will be the President of this country.' What did his teachers tell him? 'Be realistic.' If he had accepted that as reality, he would have simply been yet another ordinary American citizen. Always, Believe in your children.

On a similar vein, if A.P.J. Abdul Kalam had accepted this limited idea of immediate reality, he might never have left the small village where he was born and brought up. India might never have had this great scientist as one of its finest Presidents.

Hundreds of successful people have got to the top by refusing to listen when they were told to 'be realistic.' They've had faith in their abilities and been ready to follow their dreams and see the possibilities in life. If you want your children to believe in themselves, you have to believe in them first. However well or badly your children are doing, gives you no reason to think they can't fulfil their potential to the fullest. Any child can do wonders. Allow them to dream big.

SUMMARY OF CHAPTER 81/ XII

What's true for you may not apply to your children. Negative beliefs about abilities can restrict their potential. Children are sensitive to parental attitudes; projecting limitations can hinder their confidence. Encourage them to embrace their unique skills and chase their dreams, just as you once did. Support their aspirations without the constraints of "realism." Help them believe in possibilities.

Secret No. 81

The world overflows with endless possibilities. Nothing is impossible! Encourage your children to have colorful dreams. Don't clip their wings, let them fly high and trust in their dreams.

82

SHOULD MY CHILDREN HAVE A ROLE MODEL?

A transformative fact I have understood through my Neuro-Linguistic Programming (NLP) classes is that life is too short to commit all the mistakes ourselves and still learn. In any profession where you want to be successful, choosing a role model is the shortest route.

If your children want to be successful golfers, they could choose Tiger Woods as a role model. This means not only watching his game but also learning more about his life. If they don't delve deep into Tiger Woods' life, they'll get the impression that his success is owing to destiny!

An inspiring fact I have learned about Tiger Woods is that he spends over sixteen hours a day practicing, thinking about, and literally breathing golf. This story gives children a fresh perspective on what makes someone an achiever. It is not luck, but strategic planning and deliberate actions lead to success. By modeling their lives on those of successful individuals, children can better learn what it takes to succeed in their own chosen paths.

Parents play an essential role in guiding children to select suitable role models. An important insight is that children can learn different aspects from various people across different fields. For instance, to adopt the mindset and habits of financially successful individuals, I personally model myself after investment legends like Warren Buffet, Robert Kiyosaki of "Rich Dad, Poor Dad" fame, and the renowned Tony Robbins. Each offers unique strengths, and I aim to learn the best from all of them.

Encourage your children to delve into the lives of successful people. Many achievers have books or videos about them that can be explored as a hobby. This will offer children a different perspective on life and help them achieve their goals more quickly.

Selecting the right role model significantly affects how children shape their lives. Once they have a role model, they will adopt many useful habits and behavior patterns from them. Thus, there is one more person who communicates with your children every day and helps to steer them in the right direction.

SUMMARY OF CHAPTER 82/ XII

Understanding the value of role models is crucial for success. Children aspiring to be golfers, like Tiger Woods, should study not just techniques but his disciplined lifestyle. Parents should guide them in choosing diverse role models. Learning from successful individuals through books and videos fosters useful habits and perspectives for achieving goals.

Secret No. 82

An appropriate role model often suggests how dreams may become reality. Help your children select a positive role model they admire and are inspired by.

83

IS PARENTING FUN OR A PAIN?

What do you think of parenting? As a parent, do you feel any of the following?

- That you lack time for yourself.
- That you are overwhelmed.
- That you have to make a lot of compromises in life.
- That you are frustrated.
- That parenting is a boring job.
- That parenting is a burden.
- That parenting is a responsibility from which you can't escape.
- That parenting is a tough job.

NOW, I would like to ask you what applies to you from the following list.

- That being a parent is fun.
- It feels great.
- Your dreams are being fulfilled.
- There's lot to learn.
- You have a sense of satisfaction.
- You have a feeling of pride.

Which list suits you the best?

As a parent, you may sometimes have negative feelings, but if they are too frequent, it means that it's time to alert yourself and reflect. You have made a very important choice to be a parent, and you have children. if you constantly feel that parenting is tough, what kind of things will you do? Maybe you'll lose your temper often or run away from the responsibility.

If you consider parenting as fun, and have positive feelings about what kind of things will you do? What feelings are going to help to stand by it. You have decided to take up the responsibility of bringing As a parent you may sometimes have negative feelings, but if they you bring up children as responsible citizens with a positive attitude? You know the answer.

SUMMARY OF CHAPTER 83/ XII

Parenting can evoke both negative and positive feelings. Challenges like feeling overwhelmed or frustrated can arise, but also joy and pride. Reflecting on your emotions and finding positivity helps in raising responsible, happy children while navigating parenting's complexities.

Secret No. 83

Keep a photograph of your spouse, your children, and you, with the words 'I love parenting' on it, in your wallet. Look at it several times a day, say the words to yourself, and make this a part of your daily thought pattern.

84

THEY STEAL, TELL LIES, COME HOME LATE THERE'S A REASON BEHIND IT

What do you do when you catch your children telling lies? It could be about something they did at school or something that happened at home. Sometimes it could be a very big lie about an important assignment at school.

Are your children stealing money?

As a parent, I know your first reaction is great shock. I am sure you cannot digest the fact that the children you trust so much are actually lying or stealing. How does one handle this?

But you need to understand that children are very young. Children hear. many stories, most of which are fiction. So, when they are very young, they also learn to make up stories about what's happening, without realising the fact that they're talking about real incidents. In the real world these stories are called lies! They don't understand the significance of what they're doing.

When parents catch their children lying for the first time, it's natural for them to be upset and angry. Some parents start scolding them. As a punishment, sometime they may even stop talking to the children.

If the children are very young, you can explain to them the difference between stories and real-life incidents, but if children have outgrown that age, what can you do? If you get angry and start punishing the children, they may start withdrawing from you. They may start leaving you out of their life. In that case, you may find it really difficult to approach them later.

How can you help them? Firstly, you need to understand why they are lying. Is there a reason behind it? Normally, children lie in order to avoid punishment, to avoid doing tasks they don't like, or sometimes simply to gain attention. Usually, adolescent children start lying in order to protect their privacy and because of their fear of losing their independence.

Find out the reason for your children's lies — There is probably a positive intention behind their actions.

As a parent, what can you do to help your children?

1. You must be very honest with their school and teacher. Stop encouraging them/teaching them to tell lies, for instance, giving false reasons for their absence from school.
2. When they lie, you must express your disapproval, but you also have to make them understand that you love them very much although they have told a lie. It's their behaviour that you dislike, not them.

3. Check whether you're burdening them with too many rules, which are forcing them to lie, e.g., like a father who gave an hour-wise time table to the daughter to follow ,the daughter has no other choice but to lie, because of the fear factor.
4. Always praise children when they tell the truth. It's extremely important to talk to them to find out the real reason behind their lies.
5. Discussing the various connotations and consequences of lying will help your children to grow into honest adults.

SUMMARY OF CHAPTER 84/ XII

When discovering children lie, first assess their age and understanding. Children may mix fiction with reality, while older kids might lie to avoid punishment or guard privacy. Approach the situation with honesty, love, and support & evaluate the rules, praise honesty, and discuss consequences. Aim for open communication to foster trust and understanding.

Secret No. 84

Even if you see worrying signs, especially compulsive lying, do not give up on your children. There is probably a good reason behind these actions. Understand your children's motivations, understand them and give them your time.

85

ELEVEN OF THE MOST POPULAR QUESTIONS CHILDREN HAVE ASKED ME: MY ANSWERS AND WHAT YOU CAN LEARN FROM THEM

1. *Why do I have to study? (most popular question from children)*
   It's your life! Use it to educate you and learn wonderful new things about the world. You're not studying for your parent's or teacher's sake; you're studying for yourself!
2. *Why do my parents always compare me with my friends?*
   They want to push you, but unfortunately, your parents may not know the right way to do it. They feel you are the most capable human being, and if it is possible for anyone, it's definitely possible for you to do better. They know their child!
3. *Why don't my parents trust me?*
   How do you know they don't trust you? And if you feel strongly they don't trust you, it is up to you to create more

trust. If you want more freedom to do what you want, you also have to take more responsibility for your life.

4. *Why do my parents love my brother or sister more than me?*
   No parent can do that! Every parent does their best to love their child as much as possible. Sometimes, it's tough for a parent to ensure that every child feels the same way about. their love and affection. You must understand that your brother or sister might feel the same sometimes.
5. *Is my memory poor?*
   What makes you ask this? Every child's memory is very powerful. There is no such thing as poor memory. It's either trained or untrained memory.
6. *When my friends tease me and call me names, what should I do?*
   You must feel sure of who you are. Never feel hurt; you can't handle it that way. Either be firm and respond, or ignore them! Once you ignore them, they lose the fun of teasing you!
7. *Why do people give up their dreams so easily?*
   When young, everyone has huge dreams. Later, the hard realities of life push them to a point where they just about spend their time in this world surviving. If you need to achieve your dream, you must know that dreams are hard to follow! And the more complex the task, the greater the joy of accomplishment. But it would help if you were committed to what you want in your life to win it.

8. *Why is my teacher so unfair?*
   Your teachers will be unfair, not because they want to be so, but because they have no choice. Accept this and still find out how to excel in your school!
9. *My parents never listen to me! What should I do?*
   Think of a time when you were sick. Were your mom and dad there with you? If they never listened to you, how was this possible? Sometimes, they don't listen to you. They think they can guide you in the right direction through their experience in life because they don't want you to make the same mistakes as they did.
10. *How can I stop my mom from nagging?*
    Simple. Do your job before she asks!
11. *My parents always want to oversee what I do. I want more freedom.*
    If parents get that assurance that you are focused and sure of what you want, they would never insist on overseeing you. Your parents too need a lot of freedom. It is also painful for them to keep checking what you do!

Give them the assurance that you are focused and demonstrate how you can get great results; you will enjoy more and more freedom.

SUMMARY OF CHAPTER 85/ XII

Studying enriches your life and broadens your understanding; it's for your benefit. Parents compare you because they believe in your potential, aiming to motivate you. Trust is built through responsibility; show them you can handle freedom. Parents love equally but might struggle to express it. Memory is powerful; it's about training. When teased, stand firm or ignore it. Dreams require commitment despite life's challenges. Teachers may seem unfair due to their circumstances; focus on excelling. Parents listen through experience; demonstrate responsibility to gain freedom, reducing oversight.

Secret No. 85

Lack of communication may cause your children to see things from a negative perspective. Talk to your children and help them get rid of their wrong notions.

86

ELEVEN MYTHS ABOUT PARENTING AND WHAT YOU CAN LEARN FROM THEM

1. *Parenting is pain.*

   I have seen thousands of parents say that they think they have made a big mistake in the past by becoming parents! They say, 'It's so difficult to manage my child.' This is a total myth. You can make parenting a fun and learning experience. I always scare parents a little by suggesting that they think of the day when their children will say goodbye and leave home. Whatever the reason for their leaving, your parents will miss them terribly. You will have regrets, then. Make these days of togetherness heavenly! It is totally up to you.

2. *Teens are rebellious.*

   This is a massive generalization of teenagers. The teenage years are when children start to understand parental challenges, when they start to understand more about the realities of life, when they want to be alone when they want to become successful through their own efforts. The teenage years can be golden. It can be a time when your child supports you physically and emotionally! Make the most of this age. Whether you turn your teenage children into the most adorable individuals or rebellious teens is your choice!

3. *Positive changes take lots of time.*

   Why do most parents believe this? I have seen two common reactions in parents: If somebody says, 'I saw your child smoking!' or 'I think your child is cheating,' or 'I think your child is stealing from home,' Parents accept the information immediately and start suspecting their child. This kind of change in perception occurs instantly. I am with the parents on this one, as the parent must help the child change the negative aspects of their behavior.

   But when children experience a massive positive change, why don't parents react the same way? After our programs, I've noticed that they don't! The children always behave differently, they want to bring in a positive change. Most parents react by saying, 'Let's see how long this lasts!' This is the worst thing a parent can do! You must be willing to accept that positive changes also happen instantly and are permanent!Changes happen fast, whether positive or negative!

4. *I must not hide anything from my child.*

   If something from your past will negatively impact your children's minds, you don't have to tell them about it. When you are about to share any information, always check if it is helpful! Not whether it is true or false. Is it useful? Some examples of information that may not be always useful:

When I was young, I always used to fight with my parents. I used to cheat my teachers.

5. *I always know more because I am experienced.*

   My primary source of learning how we can modify our program to give the best to the participants is through the children and their parents attending our training programs. I want to convey that Even though I train thousands of children from various parts of the world, I never want to believe that I know more than the parents and children themselves. This is what gives me a cutting edge in my learning.

   Be ready to learn from your children. Your experience may or may not be relevant to their lives! Listen to your children's ideas. They may be new, full of potential, and better suit their lives.

6. *Once my children reach a particular age, I must behave as their friend.*

   I have seen several parents proudly saying this! Remember, your children can have any number of friends and can easily choose them, but they can have only you as a parent. This is important because when being friends, parents don't convey their feelings when their children are involved in activities that are not useful. Remember, you are always the guiding force, whatever the age of your children.

   You can always be firm and strict with lots of love. Friends cannot do this; only parents can.

7. *If my children are not ready to listen, I cannot talk to them.*

   How do you know your children are not listening? Is it because of the way they sit? The expression on their faces?

That is your interpretation of their behavior. It isn't a matter of the children listening; it's always about the parent being inflexible about communicating only in a way that seems 'fit.' I'm not saying this to blame parents; it's to make parents take stock of the situation and communicate accordingly.

8. *You'll have no freedom once you become a parent.*
   It is actually the other way around. What I have seen is that people find more ways to enjoy their freedom once they become parents. People redefine what they think of as freedom!
   I have asked people who are not yet parents what freedom means to them. The answers include going to parties late at night, spending time the way they want, traveling without anybody to trouble or nag them, and so on.
   I have asked people who are parents what freedom means to them. The answers are spending more time with their family, teaching the children, traveling with them, ensuring they are with the family during essential times, and so on. My question is, which type of freedom is more rewarding? Which will add more meaning to your life? Being a parent changes your definition of freedom.
9. *Parents must never argue in front of their children*
   If you don't want your children to learn anything about the realities of life, never say in front of your children.I have seen children who are scared when their parents argue and who have asked me questions like, 'Are they going to divorce each other?' Later, they always feel ecstatic when the parents return to their normal selves.

Let your children understand what marriage means. Arguing is a healthy part of any relationship. "By being able to disagree lovingly and not hiding it from your children, you're teaching them how to resolve conflicts healthily," says Steve Tuber, a professor of clinical psychology at the Graduate Center City College in New York City.

But remember, you mustn't have fights that are emotionally or physically abusive, and you mustn't fight about your children in front of them.

10. *Whatever the teacher says must be true!*

I have seen several children turn helpless whenever the teacher reports to their parents things like, 'Your child is very restless. Your child is slow. Your child bullies others. Your child has an attention deficit problem. Your child's memory is poor.' Parents believe the teacher.

I am not saying that you must discard what the teacher says. You need to understand that this is a time when your child needs maximum support to prove that the teacher is wrong. Remember, every action of your child has a reason.

The child is restless. It may be that he feels unsure about himself in school.

The child is slow. The teacher might not have explained things in a way that the child understood.The child bullies others. He may be assertive and stand up for his rights. It may not hurt others, but it proves that he is strong!

The child has an attention deficit problem. The subject isn't taught in an interesting way that enables him to concentrate. The child's memory is poor. The child has yet to be trained to have a good memory. There is no such thing as a poor memory. It's all about using the right strategies to remember. Respect what the teacher says, support your child emotionally, and teach him useful strategies instead of just following what the teacher says and reprimanding him.

11. *My children will take me for granted if I am not strict.*
    Untrue. If you are strict, force your children to do certain activities. Once you are off the scene, they stop. You must be firm and always ensure that your children understand the purpose of your actions.

SUMMARY OF CHAPTER 86/ XII

Parenting is often viewed as painful, leading many to regret their decision to have children. However, parenting can be a joyful journey that fosters growth and connection. Contrary to the stereotype, teenagers can be supportive and insightful rather than rebellious. Positive changes in behavior can happen quickly, yet parents often doubt these changes while accepting negative reports immediately. Parents don't always need to share every detail of their past with their children, focusing instead on useful information.

Experience doesn't mean knowing more; parents can learn valuable lessons from their children. Parents should maintain their role as guides rather than friends, providing the necessary structure. Communication is key, as perceived inattention from kids can stem from rigid methods rather than genuine disinterest.

Becoming a parent can redefine freedom, shifting focus from individual desires to family time. Arguing in front of children can teach conflict resolution, but should not involve abuse. Parents should question teachers' assessments of their children, recognizing underlying issues. Lastly, being strict doesn't guarantee respect; fostering understanding of purpose is essential for meaningful guidance.

Secret No. 86

To be a good parent, you must always have a positive attitude and mindset.

CHAPTER XIII

EXAM MINDSET AND STUDY SKILLS

If you've ever watched your child stare at a mountain of textbooks and sigh, you know that exams can feel overwhelming. But what if we could help them see tests not as threats, but as opportunities to shine and grow?

"Exam Mindset and Study Skills" is all about giving kids the confidence, habits, and tools they need to face exams with a clear head and a steady heart. Think of it as packing their backpack not just with notes and pens, but with resilience and optimism.

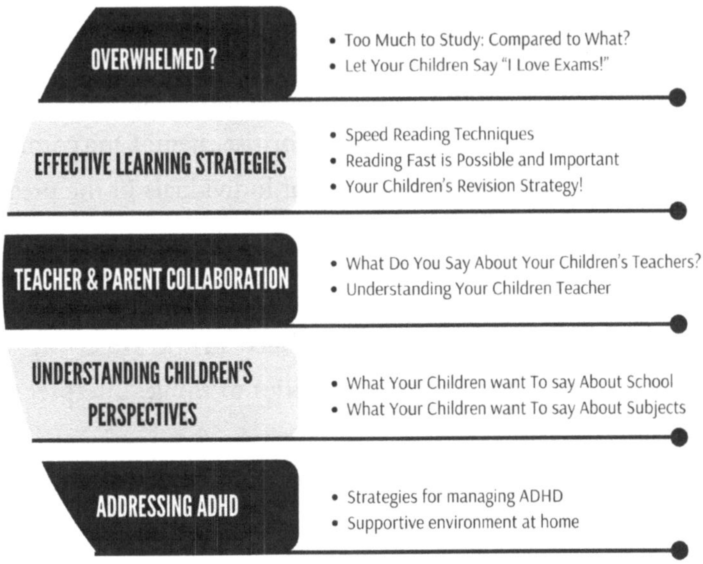

87

TOO MUCH TO STUDY: COMPARED TO WHAT?

It's a popular notion of parents, children, and several societies across the world nowadays, that studying has become too much for children, and 1 often hear parents say, 'The school syllabus is growing incredibly huge.' Both parents and children accept this as a fact. I've often heard concerned parents complain that their children have to carry really heavy bags to school!

Whenever you felt overwhelmed with work, what did you do? How many days did you waste because you felt there were lots of things to do and it was difficult to prioritise them? One common feeling that retards the productivity of individuals in the present day, is this overwhelmed feeling.

If you repeatedly tell your children that studying is too much for them, they start feeling overwhelmed in the same way and this invariably slows down their abilities to think, interpret and understand .

Let us take a few minutes and understand the following facts:

What might be impeding them is a lack of knowledge of the techniques needed to learn and remember effectively.

Now, if I ask you, what do you think of your children's capability to store, process and recall information, I can almost hear you agree that it is AMAZING! So, stop telling them, 'Your syllabus is huge.' How will they study then? Their syllabus is tiny compared to the number of neurons they have at their command and their consequent capability. Being able to see their syllabus as manageable, will undoubtedly give your children a sense of control. Don't worry on their behalf, remember:

Your children Piave a huge capacity to understand.

SUMMARY OF CHAPTER 87/ XIII

Secret No. 87

Children possess remarkable mental capacity, often greater than we realize, so there's no need to worry excessively about their workload. Their syllabus is manageable compared to the cognitive tools they have. Encourage them with confidence, avoiding any suggestion that their schoolwork and activities are overwhelming.

88

READING FAST IS POSSIBLE AND IMPORTANT

Do you know the average reading speed of a student when they are not trained in any particular method? It's approximately about fifty to seventy five words a minute. Stop right here because this is slow and much below the brain's capacity.

Your brain is capable of processing much more information per minute. What prevents us from achieving a higher reading speed is the belief that reading fast will reduce comprehension. Is that true?

Research shows that the brain can absorb information more easily if it's grouped into meaningful chunks. If you read a group of words at a time, it can result in reducing your reading time and, at the same time, result in better comprehension. So reading fast becomes very important for better comprehension.

When a person reads very slowly, their mind wanders, and they end up reading the same words again and again. Speed reading can overcome this problem by making you more focused.

When you drive a car very slowly, say at 15 kilometers an hour, how do you feel? You may be talking over the phone or looking around at new constructions that are coming up. But what will your focus be if you're driving the same car at a higher speed, say a hundred kilometers per hour? It has to be on your driving. The mind works that way. You need to totally engage the brain to gather the concentration to do that.

Once you start reading very fast, it not only reduces the time taken but improves your comprehension capabilities. It also increases your concentration. There are various ways in which you can improve your reading speed. For example, you could use a pencil or a pen as a guide to avoid your mind wandering.

Playing fast music in the background can also increase reading speed because it cuts off other associated thoughts. An example of an associated thought is when you read the term 'water,' you think of 'beach.' Similar associations slow down your reading speed considerably.

The ideas I've mentioned above have powerful effects on increasing the reading speed of children, if put into practice.

SUMMARY OF CHAPTER 88/ XIII

The average reading speed for untrained students is 50-75 words per minute, below the brain's capacity. This slow pace can hinder comprehension. Research shows that grouping words into chunks enhances understanding and speeds up reading. Techniques like using a guide or playing fast music can improve focus and accelerate reading speed effectively.

Secret No. 88

Teach children that reading faster enhances comprehension and focus by allowing the brain to process information in meaningful chunks. Encourage the use of tools like a pencil for guidance and techniques such as playing fast music to minimize distractions. Reassure them of their brain's capability to process information efficiently, boosting their confidence in reading speed and retention.

89

YOUR CHILDREN'S REVISION STRATEGY

As parent, you need to realize that your involvement in your children's duration is crucial to their eventual success. Surprisingly, the results of research indicate that one factor that significantly affects a child's success in school is parental involvement, especially during the preparation for exams.

One of the most significant steps in the process of being successful in an examination is, having the right strategies for revision. When revising, children commonly spend a lot of time on a few chapters to start with, and later start worrying about how little time they have, to complete the rest of their syllabus. Because of this, they end up cramming during the day (and often, the night) before the exam. Parents can play a very important role here in helping their children to plan effectively, so that they cover all the work they need to do, as well as check with them periodically to see how it's going.

Recent research studies show that in order to retain things in our long-term memory, and for effective recall during examinations, revision must happen a minimum four times. The first revision, within a few hours of learning, can help the child retain eighty per cent of what they have learnt. The second revision should be done after twenty-four hours, the third, after a week and the fourth, after a month. This makes the learning stay permanently imprinted in the memory.

As its biggest challenge during revision is a lack of time, many strategies have been developed for more efficient revision. One such strategy includes identifying key words and linking them using your imagination to make a story, or seeing pictures and making mindmaps. *(Mindmap – A trademark of Tony Buzan)*

Mindmap is powerful tool used to organize ideas in the right sequence Mindmaps have been proven to be very effective for faster revision and recall. Most of these techniques are available over the internet. According to Albert Einstein, 'Imagination is more powerful than knowledge.

The study environment also plays a key role in effective revision. A well lit room with a comfortable chair, and some fast music in the background will help the child focus better. Eating balanced meals and not postponing meals is a must for the child. During revision, children tend to munch on snacks between meals. Parents should make sure that these snacks aren't oily or fatty, by always keeping a selection of healthy snacks available at home.

Help your child to make an exam goal poster with the marks they expect in all their subjects and put it up in their room. This will help the child to work out effective strategies to get those marks.

Making posters for important formulae or diagrams in bright colors and sticking them on the wall also help to speed up revision.

You could also make a table of important dates and places in history on a big poster or a chart and paste it on the wall. To help remember maps in geography, the strategy is to give specific colors to different areas. For example, if they have to remember the kingdom assign a particular color to that kingdom, and also remember it through associations of shape. Everyone remembers Italy well because it's in the shape of a boot! Help your children to come up with their own strategies.

SUMMARY OF CHAPTER 89/ XIII

Parental involvement is vital for children's academic success, especially during exam preparation. Effective revision strategies are crucial; children often mismanage time, causing last-minute cramming. Encouraging regular revisions, using techniques like mind maps, and creating an optimal study environment improves retention. Healthy snacks, goal posters, and visual aids enhance learning. Helping children devise personal strategies fosters independence in their study habits.

Secret No. 89

Encourage your children to develop intelligent strategies for adequate exam preparation. When they feel overwhelmed, remind them that they can achieve their goals and be there to support them. Your presence will help them feel ready for their exams.

90

LET YOUR CHILDREN SAY `I LOVE EXAMS'!

Are your children very scared of taking exams? Do they throw up before exams or feel nauseated? Refuse to eat breakfast? Say they can feel butterflies in their stomachs. In that case, how can you, as a parent, help your children?

It's pretty common for children to feel anxious about exams. This is a sign that they are taking the exams seriously. Your children need to feel relaxed and confident about their exams. At the time of their exams, you should also be well prepared. Ensure you know exactly what time each exam is, where it's taking place, and what's expected of your children. This will make exams a lot easier.

If your children begin to panic, teach them to tell themselves something like, 'I am calm and focused.' Simply repeating this will help them feel calmer. Visualizing the exams going well can also make your children feel more confident. If the exam is important, or your children are apprehensive, doing a practice exam at home may be a good idea.

A good night's sleep before the exam is far better than last-minute cramming. Similarly, your children must eat a balanced diet before the exams. Choose the food carefully: high-fat, sugar-and caffeine-containing foods won't optimize their brain function.

Make sure that your children arrive on time for the exam. This will be easier if you keep everything that you need handy well in advance. Rushing will only make your children feel more nervous. Always remember that your children should carry a spare pen. Some basic exam techniques will help ensure success. Remembering to read the instructions carefully will help.

Many children lose marks because they rush through writing and need to read the instructions carefully. To build confidence and potentially increase marks, it's important to allocate time for each section and start with the most accessible parts.

I've often asked large groups of children, "How many of you love your exams?" Usually, no hands go up. But when I ask, "How many hate your exams?" many hands rise with irritated expressions. The thought of exams isn't pleasant for most.

Parents often reinforce this negativity by saying, "Once your exam is over, you'll have all the freedom in the world to relax."

A key trait of all successful people I've encountered, including musicians, athletes, and business leaders, is love for what they do. Tiger Woods must love golf to be the best, and I remind myself daily that I love training people. Similarly, students need to learn to love exams if they want to perform their best.

If you are yet to get a copy of my 'I Love Exams' book do get the same immediately and also go through the course online.

SUMMARY OF CHAPTER 90/ XIII

Children often feel anxious about exams, showing signs like nausea or loss of appetite. As a parent, help them feel relaxed and confident by being well-prepared and teaching calming techniques. Encourage good sleep and a balanced diet, avoid rushing, and ensure they arrive on time. Emphasize the importance of reading instructions carefully and managing their time wisely. Ultimately, fostering a positive attitude towards exams can enhance performance.

Secret No. 90

Teach your children to say **"I LOVE EXAMS"** and gradually learn to mean it.

It will invariably have a big impact on their scores.

91

WHAT DO YOU SAY ABOUT YOUR CHILDREN'S TEACHERS?

Let me share one of my experiences which I had with an eight year old child and her parents. They were facing a serious challenge and I met them to help find a solution.

The parent described the problem in this way, "Almost every day. I'm called to school to meet the class teacher. The teacher always complains that my daughter doesn't listen to her and disturbs the class. I know that this isn't true because at home she behaves very well. Her teacher treats her differently from the other children. For some reason, the teacher doesn't like her."

When I talked to the child, the first thing she said was, 'I don't like my class teacher, and she treats me differently from the rest of my class.'

What you say to your children about the teacher is very important. Once the children start to dislike their teachers or feel that the teachers are biased, then they will start finding out different ways in which their teacher has treated them differently. I asked her why she thought so, and she made a long list.

- She always calls out my name and tells me to be quiet when everybody else in the class is talking.
- Whatever we're doing, she will call me to the front and ask me to write on the board.
- At least once a week, she threatens to take me to the Principal.
- I know she doesn't like me. She always picks on me!

I asked both the mother and the daughter, ' Is there any possibility that the teacher likes your daughter a lot and wants her to do better? Is it possible she isn't picking on her but wants to pay special attention to the child? This thought may or may not be accurate, but it will be very useful for the child.

Once your children are convinced that their teacher likes them and that's why she treats them that way, it will create a deep change in the relationship between the children and the teacher. As you know, the rapport between children and their teachers is very important for the children to participate successfully in the learning process . Once they like the teacher of a particular subject, that subject becomes a favorite subject.

SUMMARY OF CHAPTER 91/ XIII

An eight-year-old girl faced challenges with her teacher, leading her parents to seek help. The child felt singled out and disliked by the teacher, impacting her view of school. I suggested considering that the teacher might actually care about her learning, as a positive perspective could improve their relationship, fostering better engagement and success in her education.

Secret No. 91

The rapport between children and their teachers is essential for children to learn well and learn happily. What you tell your children about their teacher is very important. Look for approving interpretations of their teacher's behavior and convey the same to your children.

92

ATTENTION DEFICIT HYPERACTIVE DISORDER : FEEL IN CONTROL AND SUPPORT YOUR CHILDREN

Are your children lacking in concentration and feeling restless?

Do they throw frequent temper tantrums?

Are they highly overactive?

In short, is snaking your children to sit in one place for a little while a difficult task? In the recent past, have your children's school teachers called you for a special meeting and listed the following problems?

- Are highly inattentive in class.
- Daydream a lot.
- Don't finish their homework.
- Are very impulsive.
- Don't finish the classwork on time.

After listing all these, did the teacher drop a bombshell saying that you may have to visit a psychiatrist soon? There are also times when I have heard parents say, 'Otherwise, they may consider expelling my children from school!' I have personally witnessed the pain parents undergo after having the above-mentioned experience. They are clueless as to what they should do about it!

At times like these, you, as a parent, must control the situation and support your children. You must not have a helpless attitude, even though you might be overwhelmed with a feeling of fear. When children feel overactive and lack concentration, it may not always mean they have a medical disorder. It may also mean that:

1. *The Current Activity Is Not Interesting Enough To Capture Their Attention:* When an activity isn't interesting enough, attention spans decrease as the mind shifts to more engaging stimuli. For instance, you might stop reading the newspaper when your favorite song plays on TV. Children often face attention deficits because their activities aren't captivating. As a parent, you can support by making their learning process engaging, utilizing whole-brain methodologies. Encourage using both left and right brain functions through study tools like pictorial representations, music, and activity-oriented learning, making the experience fun and stimulating.
2. *The Capability of the Mind is much higher than the task:* When an activity isn't challenging enough, it can lead to boredom, like losing interest in simple math compared to engaging with Sudoku. To help your children manage this, teach them the value of responsibility and maintaining interest. They must understand that educational requirements cannot be changed

overnight, and staying engaged is important despite the challenge.

3. *Children are identified as having ADHD:* There are times when the parents feel that nothing is working out and decide to visit a psychiatrist. If the child is identified with ADHD — 'Attention Deficit Hyperactive Disorder,' what is it that you can do? How can you support your children as a parent? When your child is diagnosed with ADHD, maintain a positive and controlled mindset. This approach is crucial because it influences your child's future. Avoid labeling all negative behaviors as ADHD-related, as this can worsen the condition. Treat your child normally, and help them understand they can concentrate by making tasks interesting. Reinforcing this can improve their focus and reduce ADHD symptoms.

In our camps, we often have children diagnosed with ADHD. One memorable experience involved a nineteen-year-old diagnosed at seven. His behavior was definitely abnormal compared to students of his age group. He found it difficult to sit in one place; he chose an unusual body posture while sitting down, and so on. The 'fact' that he was a special child had been reinforced for several years by his environment. He was also under medication.

During the camp, however, the trainers reported certain amazing facts about him. As a part of the learning programme, children were taught how to enhance their reading speeds during the camp. The exercise goes something like this: There are lots of numbers in a row and each child must identify one specific number in that group and circle the number throughout. This is one of the difficult exercises, as it requires lot of focus and concentration.

Interestingly, this student, who was diagnosed with ADHD, performed this test extremely well and was consistently the fastest among the hundreds of other participants. My question, then, is, how did this same student display the highest level of focus? Once he found something highly challenging and interesting, his entire concentration was given to the same and he was able to sustain his focus.

SUMMARY OF CHAPTER 92/ XIII

Are your children restless, inattentive in class, or impulsive? If teachers express concerns and suggest seeing a psychiatrist, it can leave parents feeling helpless. However, it's essential to understand that such behaviors might not always indicate a medical disorder. Children might lack concentration if activities are uninteresting or too easy. Engage them with stimulating, challenging tasks and utilize whole-brain methodologies for learning. If diagnosed with ADHD, maintain a positive outlook and avoid labeling negative behaviors as ADHD-related. Reinforcing their strengths in engaging activities can enhance focus. A camp experience showed how a child thrived when given challenging, interesting tasks to tackle.

Secret No. 92

When your children lack concentration or feel restless, it may not always mean that they have a medical disorder, even though their teacher and doctor may suspect one. During those tough times, feel in control and support your children in handling this challenge in a positive way.

93

ELEVEN THINGS YOUR CHILDREN WANT TO SAY ABOUT SCHOOL AND SUBJECTS AND WHAT YOU CAN LEARN FROM THEM

The following are your children's views, which will make you see things from their perspective. They will also give you an idea of how to encourage and help them perform better in school.

1. I may have failed in certain subjects in the past. Please understand that the past doesn't necessarily equate with the future.
2. When I get confused with any of my subjects, I never think I'm incapable. Please understand that I'm learning something new.
3. When I forget a few things in some subjects, it doesn't mean my memory is poor. It only means I am yet to learn how to remember!
4. When I showed you my report card, and I had a low grad., you compared it with my friends and told me how much

worse I was. I want your unconditional love and support during the moments I feel low.

5. You told my teacher what a troublemaker I was. If there's any trouble in the class, my teacher looks at me suspiciously, although I'm in no way connected with it.
6. When my friends describe their holidays, I also want to have a story to tell. Do take me to new places; it teaches me to adapt and helps me learn more about life.
7. A specific teacher repeatedly calls me stupid in class. Last time, I avoided competing, though I actually love to participate. I want you to push me and remind me that 'There is no failure, only feedback.'
8. Mom, Dad, I beg you not to take me to a psychiatrist about any of my activities in school that may seem 'abnormal'! My abnormal behavior is that I am bored, seeking attention, or have yet to learn how to behave. It's tough for me to accept the names that a psychiatrist may give me: ADHD, LD, and so on. Keep that only as a last resort!
9. When I failed to win a prize, you encouraged me to prepare better for the next one. That is what made me win the next! I understand that you can inspire me very easily!
10. When I say that Its bored, please translate it as one of the following: I don't understand what is expected of me. The work is too easy or too difficult. I need more of a challenge!
11. When I give cases saying the subject is very difficult, do remind me that my capabilities are much higher! Whenever I say I can't do it, always tell me, 'If I can't, then I must!'

SUMMARY OF CHAPTER 93/ XIII

Children express the need for understanding and support in their academic journey. They want parents to recognize that past failures don't determine future success. Confusion is part of learning, and memory lapses indicate a need for better retention strategies. They seek unconditional love during low moments and encouragement after setbacks, desire enriching experiences beyond school, and need reassurance of their potential despite challenges and labels.

Secret No. 93

See things from your children's point of view, rather than forming an opinion based on your preset notions.

CHAPTER XIV

CREATING A POSITIVE ENVIRONMENT AT HOME

"Nurturing Home Environments for Child Well-being," presents a guide for parents on how to cultivate a supportive atmosphere within the home. It highlights the importance of such an environment for a child's emotional well-being, development, and resilience. This chapter suggests that positive parental behaviours, coupled with open dialogue and acknowledgement of individual differences, are crucial for creating a space where children can flourish. Ultimately, it describes how a nurturing home forms the bedrock for children's happiness and their capacity for learning.

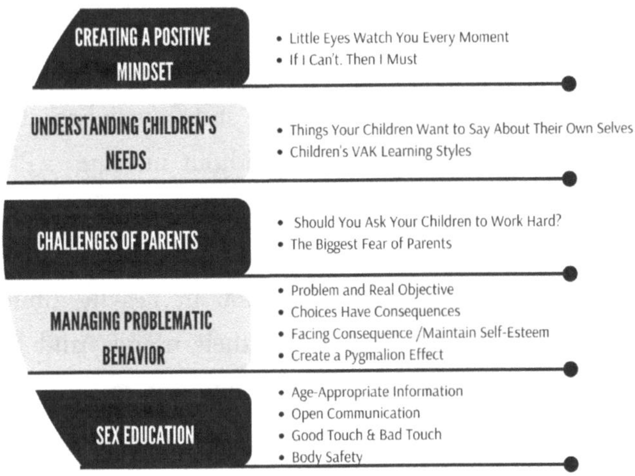

94

LITTLE EYES WATCH YOU EVERY MOMENT

Are you aware of how much parenting changes you? It brings new responsibilities, demands commitment, and can build new beliefs and a sense of drive. If approached in the right way, it transforms you positively forever. From the moment they're born, your children observe you closely, observing all your actions to replicate them later.

What shapes your children into who they are? Sociologist Morris Massey identifies three key stages of development:

1. *Age 0 to 7 – Imprinting Age:* This stage is particularly crucial, especially between the ages of two and four, when children absorb information rapidly and without filtering. . Phobias often start between ages three and seven, with further events reinforcing initial negative emotions.
2. *Age 8 to 14 – Modeling Age:* Children are heavily influenced by their surroundings and notice their friends' and heroes' behaviors.By the age of ten, children start to imitate their role models. It's important to guide them in choosing positive examples to follow.

3. *Age 14 to 21 – Socialization Age:* Children start forming close relationships beyond their parents and establish their own values. These values rarely change after twenty-one, except through intense emotional experiences or inspirational learning programs.

In each phase, who influences them the most? The parents! If you want your child to be responsible, you need to be responsible. If you want them to be committed, demonstrate commitment. If you want them to embrace empowering beliefs, you must embody these beliefs yourself. If you want them to have strong values, use those values to guide your own life.

You have the greatest influence on your children. Parenting is a wonderful chance to strive for excellence in life. Immediately after becoming a parent, you become a hero to your child. As a trainer, I've learned that people always observe what I do personally. I must serve as a role model if I want to make a positive impact. Loving my profession pushes me to be better. I am cautious about delaying tasks and being unmotivated because those in my programs look to me for inspiration. I am grateful for the opportunity to impact many lives while pushing myself to achieve more.

Parenting is an opportunity to better your own life. Remember, those young eyes always watch you, learning to mimic everything you do!

SUMMARY OF CHAPTER 94/ XIV

Parenting significantly transforms individuals, introducing new responsibilities and shaping beliefs. Children undergo three development stages: imprinting (0-7), modeling (8-14), and socialization (14-21), with parents as their primary influence. Parents must embody desired values and behaviors, as children closely observe and replicate actions. Parenting is a chance for personal growth, as children learn by watching their parents.

Secret No. 94

Allow parenting to motivate you to be at your best, knowing that your journey of excellence leads your children by example.

95

IF I CAN'T, THEN I MUST

Whenever you ask children to do something they don't like or they find difficult, the immediate answer you get is, 'I can't.' It becomes valid if you believe you can or can't do something. For example, a child believes that he can't do maths. That becomes true for that child because he is completely convinced about it.

When you want your children to do something, make it a must. That is the only way. Instill this powerful belief in your children - 'If I can't, then I must.'

We have noticed daily that many things we think we just can't do happen easily enough when they become essential. Instead of waiting for them to become urgent, can't we make them necessary right now?

Many people throughout history have made what they can't do easily a must for themselves. However difficult they've found things, whatever the obstacles they've faced, they've believed that they MUST do something, and so have succeeded. You can find examples in all walks of life, amongst all kinds of people.

One person who has inspired me a lot is Oprah Winfrey, the multiple-award-winning host of The Oprah Winfrey Show, the highest-rated talk show in television history.

Let me share her story with you.

One person who has inspired me throughout my life is Oprah Winfrey. Oprah hosts the most popular talk show of all time, 'The Oprah Winfrey Show,' which is one of the highest-rated shows in television history.

Oprah Winfrey, renowned for hosting "The Oprah Winfrey Show," the most popular talk show in TV history, has been a lifelong inspiration to many. Born in Mississippi to unmarried teenagers, Her mother, Vernita Lee, was, at that point, a housemaid, and her father, Vernon Winfrey, worked in a coal mine. She spent her early years in poverty with her strict grandmother. Her grandma used to hit her with a switch if she didn't finish her chores or if she misbehaved. When she was six, Oprah started living with her mother, who was less supportive than her grandmother. She did not have a very healthy childhood and was even molested by a cousin and a family friend.

Even in the face of these many adversities, Oprah did not let all these factors become an excuse for innumerable excuses and cant's. Instead, she managed to do well in her studies, found a mentor, and got a scholarship when she was thirteen years old. Later, because of the numerous problems at home, she ran away. When she was thirteen, she was sent to a juvenile detention home. Later, she moved to Nashville with Vernon, her father. Though Vernon was strict, he was encouraging and paid close attention to her education.Today, people envy her lifestyle because of her popularity. Time magazine identified her as one of the 100 most influential people of the 20th century. Oprah turned all her can' ts into a must.

If your child says, 'I can't learn science,' make it a 'must' to help your child come up with a strategy to learn science.

If your child says, 'I can't write well,' then it is a 'must' that you help your child learn how to write well!

SUMMARY OF CHAPTER 95/ XIV

Children often respond with "I can't" when faced with difficult tasks, becoming true to their beliefs. To shift this mindset, instill a must mentality: "If I can't, then I must." Throughout history, many have succeeded by transforming challenges into essentials. Oprah Winfrey exemplifies this, overcoming a troubled childhood filled with adversity to become a highly influential figure. Instead of succumbing to obstacles, she thrived through education and mentorship, showing that with determination, what seems impossible can become a necessity.

Secret No. 95

Teaching children to view challenges as opportunities for growth can help them build resilience. Encouraging a mindset of determination can empower them to overcome adversities.

96

THE BIGGEST FEAR OF PARENTS

What is the biggest fear that parents have when it comes to their children? All parents answer that it's their concern for their children's future. The question that parents always have in mind is whether their children will be successful in life. As parents, this is their biggest responsibility. Because of this fear, parents start worrying when they notice that their children are engaged in certain not-so-useful activities.

There is no guarantee that the parents will be there with the children throughout their lives to guide them. This means that the children will have to face the world alone at some point, sooner or later.

Fearing this fact, parents do their best to help their children cease from any activity they do not approve of. That is when they go and shout at their children, punish them. Doing this means that sometimes the parents feel bad about the negative feelings they evoke in their children. But they believe that if they refrain from their duty, just because they don't want to upset them, the children will never know where they have to correct themselves.

If you look at this from the children's perspective, the children will never readily understand the deep love behind a parent's behaviour. They will keep thinking that it's a habit of their parents to nag, or that their parents take pride in doing so.

In fact, that's when they answer hack, saying things like, 'Why are you always after my life? Leave me alone.' To avoid being seen and subsequently stopped by their parents, they may start doing things secretively.

One such incident was shared by a mother in one of our camps.

Her daughter had been spending lot of time on her mobile phone. So the mother imposed certain restrictions on its use. She was under the impression that the child has listened to her advice. One day when she entered her daughter's room, she was under the impression that her daughter was sleeping, but when she took the bed sheet off she saw her daughter whispering very quietly into her mobile phone. She was shocked to see this and wondered why it had happened.

SUMMARY OF CHAPTER 96/ XIV

The biggest fear parents have is their children's future success. Concerned about negative activities, parents sometimes resort to shouting and punishment, which can create negative feelings. Children, lacking understanding of parental love, may see it as nagging and respond defensively. A mother discovered her daughter secretly using her phone despite restrictions, highlighting the challenges in communication.

Secret No. 96

Whenever you find your children resist your advice or answer back, it is time for you to sit with them and share your concerns in the nicest possible way. You'll find that their response to this truth will be one of understanding. You can work out a solution together.

97

SHOULD YOU ASK YOUR CHILDREN TO WORK HARD

I've often asked children and adults that what they think the formula for being successful in life is. More than half of those I ask, say hard work! Well, its laborers who work that hard to earn their bread. Of course hard work is important to be successful but it alone can't be treated as a complete recipe for success. To be highly successful you need to think differently, think smart!

If you look around you, you'll find that most of the highly successful people, didn't just work hard but they dared to do things differently and refused to be a part of the 'rat-race!

Teaching your children always to work hard will create two possible frames of mind:

1.If they start getting results, they begin to believe that the only way to achieve anything in life is by working hard! So, even though they turn out to be dedicated, hard-working individuals, they may not be able to balance their lives between work and extracurricular activities.

2. If they are unable to produce results even after working hard, they will most likely start feeling frustrated. Some might work even harder. However, most will start believing that being successful or outstanding in life is a very tough task. This may cause them to give up on things quickly and stop doing new things. This frame of mind may instill in them a fear of failure.

Neither of the above mindsets is useful. As a parent, should you never tell your children to work hard or help them develop the habit of working hard? No! But in addition to that, there's something more important: you should tell your children to "Think smart." Start saying it now!

SUMMARY OF CHAPTER 97/ XIV

Success isn't solely about hard work but also about thinking differently and smartly. Teaching children only the importance of hard work can lead to unbalanced lives or frustration. Encouraging them to think smart alongside hard work fosters a more balanced, innovative approach to success.

Secret No. 97

If your children want to improve in the race of life, they must learn to think smart.

98

YOUR CHILDREN'S VAK SKILLS

I can share some of the most powerful tips with you to ensure that your children use all of their senses while learning. For instance, notes for every chapter should be created in a visually appealing way, such as using pictures. I'm sure your children will learn more quickly this way!

When children are young and in the first few years of their schooling, their learning is always very rapid, and they're excited about their studies. Almost every child loves their school rhymes and the teachers who teach them. When do subjects turn challenging? As the children grow older! What is the primary reason that children learn more slowly as they grow up? How do they learn when they're young?

Think about how you learned nursery rhymes as a young child. Whether children memorize a set of words alone or add rhythm and actions, they use all the senses they can—visual (V), auditory (A), and kinesthetic (K). When all these senses are used, learning is faster and more thorough. Children remember better this way.

Textbooks transform. When children start learning, their books are filled with pictures and minimal writing, appearing colorful.

Every line is supported by pictures and illustrations. However, between the ages of eight and ten, the number of pictures decreases while the text increases. By the time they are twelve to fifteen, illustrations become black and white and are fewer, with most being technical. After the age of fifteen, illustrations become rare in textbooks. Unfortunately, music and rhymes mostly disappear from their studies. Rules are often set by parents and teachers that music should not be part of study time, which never gets included in their study routine.

To maintain high enthusiasm for studying, encourage your children to use all their senses in the learning process:

1. Visual: Stimulate the visual element by making notes creatively, using sketches, colors, and diagrams.
2. Auditory: Encourage children to record themselves reading answers and play them back. They can also make rhythms to remember sequences. These techniques make learning fun and engaging.
3. Kinesthetic: Incorporate actions in learning, which uses the theory of association. Although some children might feel self-conscious about using actions, associating it with childishness, it is actually a very effective learning method.

SUMMARY OF CHAPTER 98/ XIV

As a parent, enhance your child's learning by engaging all their senses. Create visually appealing notes using pictures, encourage recording and playback of readings, and incorporate actions for kinesthetic learning. Early education features vibrant visuals and rhymes, which diminish later. To maintain excitement, emphasize creativity, rhythm, and movement in their study routine for more effective retention.

Secret No. 98

All senses should be utilized in the learning process. Help your children develop this holistic approach.

99

THE IMPORTANCE OF GIVING YOUR CHILDREN SEX EDUCATION

Even though parents often want to tell their children more about sex, the social rules stop them. This chapter will focus on providing answers to the most burning thoughts and questions that parents have about sex and will concentrate on how they should educate their children about the same. The world over, one of the most debatable topics is 'Whether the children should learn about sex by themselves or should they be taught?'

Look at it this way: children never learn about sex by themselves. They are taught the same either by television or movies, certain websites, or society in general. Even your unspoken words educate them, unfortunately, usually in the wrong way. How many children today watch 'Adults Only' certified content either in the Cinema Hall or on TV? All of them! Hence, as a parent, you play a huge role in streamlining those thoughts.

As a parent, you must understand that sex is neither dirty nor a sin. Never think that when your children show curiosity to learn more about the topic, it is a total waste of time. It is a human instinct, and all children go through this natural phase of growth. Do accept the fact that your children are growing up. Interestingly, research studies say that children start developing the instinct to know about the bodily differences between men and women as early as four years of age. Never hate this thought; it only means that your children are experiencing the right mental and emotional maturity.

1. When your children are curious about the birth-process, never make up stories that are not true, stories such as 'God put the child in mom's stomach or one day we found your brother/ sister from the sky, etc.' Simplify the process of birth as per the age of your children.
2. Never avoid topics when your little one asks questions about the human body or the difference between the body of a girl and a boy. If you don't help them find the right answers, they will end up having the wrong assumptions. The aim is simplifying the idea and help them to understand the facts. Never inculcate thoughts like women are generally weak and men are strong. It has a lifelong negative effect on the health of the female child or an incorrect perception of women for a male child.
3. Stop telling stereotypes or general rules based on gender, like 'Men are unfaithful,' 'Women talk a lot,' 'Men are selfish,' etc. They are not true and tend to hurt your children's mindset.
4. It is highly unintelligent to take your children to movies with high adult content. Certain movies portray highly wrong notions about sex and the natural attraction between men and

women. At times, the feeling is magnified several times, and such a scene proves to be highly disturbing for the mind. As a parent, you are responsible for avoiding taking your children to such movies.

5. Nowadays, children have access to adult content at the touch of a button, be it on the internet or on their mobile phones. Avoid keeping the internet in a secluded corner of your house, and make sure you install some web screening software, which automatically prevents the appearance of websites that are not children's friendly.
6. Research studies have time and again proved that teenage children look for closer or abnormal relationships with the opposite sex primarily because of one of two factors:
   - Family values are not deeply inculcated.
   - They find few opportunities to share their feelings and emotions with someone at home.

As a parent, you are responsible for taking cam of both these areas. Do help your children understand the marriage system and the sanctity associated with the same. Never miss an opportunity to explain to your children some of the interesting rituals and procedures followed in a marriage by different cultures and religions. As your children enter into their teen years, it becomes highly important to spend mom quality time with them. It is important to ensure that you create a platform where they feel comfortable sharing their challenges regarding relationships with you and older and more mature family members.

If the societal norms don't openly allow you to teach your children about sex, make sure you are the guiding force. Remember, you have all the rights and responsibilities to guide your children in the right direction.

SUMMARY OF CHAPTER 99/ XIV

Parents often feel constrained by social norms when discussing sex with their children. This chapter emphasizes the necessity of educating children about sex rather than leaving them to learn from potentially misleading sources like media and society. It's crucial for parents to realize that curiosity about sex is natural, starting as early as age four. Rather than resorting to false narratives about birth, parents should answer questions honestly. Stereotypes and adult content should be avoided to prevent negative perceptions. Research shows that teenagers may seek inappropriate relationships due to a lack of family values and communication. Engaging in open discussions about marriage and relationships fosters healthy understanding and trust.

Secret No. 99

If you don't make efforts to educate your children about sex, they will turn to the media or society for the same. This may lead them to make wrong assumptions. As a parent, you are responsible for ensuring your children learn the correct facts about human birth, the relationship between men and women, sex, and moral values.

100

ELEVEN THINGS YOUR CHILDREN WANT TO SAY ABOUT THEIR OWN SELVES, AND WHAT YOU CAN LEARN FROM THEM

Parents sometimes curb their children's growth by not giving them enough space or by not letting them take their own decisions. The following are your children's views. If you keep them in mind, you will be better able to help your children in their personal growth.

1. I want to be independent, but understand that I need your support sometimes.
2. When I come home, sometimes I may not respond to your questions. Please understand that I need some time and space for myself and that this isn't a sign of disrespect.
3. I may refuse to take up certain activities that you suggest, like learning music or playing tennis. Just understand that I am different.

4. Please remember that your actions. have greater impact than your words. If you want me to attend my classes regularly, please show the same kind of discipline with your activities!
5. Never compare. Usually it puts me down and makes me think I am less capable than my friends! Do I ever compare you with my friends' parents?
6. 1 took money without your permission, not because I wanted to steal, but because I misunderstood and thought that only when 1 spend a lot of money will my friends respect me. Please understand and help me to change..
7. When I was explaining why I couldn't finish my homework, you interrupted and started yelling at me. If only you'd listen...
8. Never think that by not getting angry with me, you are a good parent. In fact, then you are a bad parent. Act naturally!
9. When I'm sick, don't do all my jobs. It makes me feel comfortable, and it will be really difficult for me to suddenly come out of it. It sometimes makes me think I should get sick again to enjoy that incredible love and comfort you shower on me!
10. If you want to know things about me ask me directly. before you talk to anyone else. I understand that I can trust you always.
11. Never decide who I am by looking at my mistakes. Doesn't everyone make mistakes?

SUMMARY OF CHAPTER 100/ XIV

Parents may unintentionally limit their children's growth by not allowing independence or space. Children express the desire for support while needing time alone, individuality, and respect. They highlight the importance of actions over words, dislike comparisons, and seek understanding for mistakes. Listening and direct communication foster trust, while avoiding judgment encourages healthier development and relationships.

Secret No. 100

Every child's circumstances are different.See the difference and accept it.

101

THE ULTIMATE FORMULA TO MANAGE PROBLEMATIC BEHAVIOUR!

In The modern world, raising teenagers is no easy task. It's simple for parents and kids to feel lost in the midst of shifting emotions, increasing independence, and social pressures. But what if your parenting journey could be guided by a methodical approach, a straightforward yet effective formula?

The four main pillars of The Ultimate Success Formula for Parents are intended to enable you and your child to develop through difficulties rather than around them.

Step 1: Recognize the True Issue

Take a moment to connect before you correct. There is a deeper reason behind every behavior your child displays. Is your teenager misbehaving, avoiding responsibilities, or withdrawing? Take your time fixing the surface. Rather, ask yourself: What is the true problem?truly attempting to accomplish, even if they're approaching it incorrectly. Every grievance and misbehavior stems from a need for autonomy, security, or attention. Finding the main issue makes your response much more insightful.

Step 2: Choices Have Consequences

The decisions your child makes will affect their future, but only if they are aware that every decision has an impact.The compelling notion that people live up to expectations is known as the Pygmalion Effect. Your child will often fit your perception of them as being unmotivated, careless, or unyielding. However, they are more likely to become that version if you believe in their transformation.

"I know this is not who you really are," you should say to your teen. I think you've changed.

Step 3: Allow them to accept the result without diminishing their value as individuals

Seeing our kids make mistakes is difficult. However, protecting them from every hiccup in the road doesn't get them ready for what lies ahead.Let them deal with the consequences. Allow them to experience the repercussions of staying up late or failing to finish a task. However, and this is very important, never allow them to feel inferior as a result.

"You made a mistake," you say. However, I am aware that this is not who you are. I still have faith in you.That equilibrium between responsibility and unwavering respect? It is the foundation of self-esteem.

Step 4: Have faith in their future selves

Do you know what the Pygmalion Effect is? It's the notion that people turn into what other people think they should be. And it's very real, particularly when it comes to kids.If we keep telling our child, "You're always careless," they might just live up to that label. But if we say, "I know you can handle this. I trust you," they'll rise to that, too.Teenagers may roll their eyes, but deep down, they want to know we still see the good in them. They need our belief more than they admit.

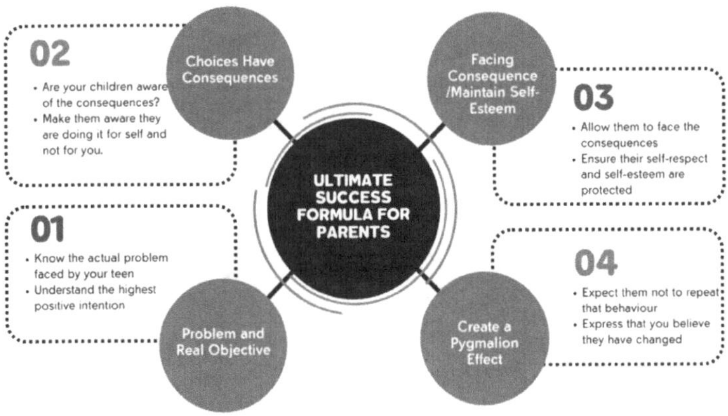

SUMMARY OF CHAPTER 101/ XIV

This chapter focuses on the Ultimate Success Formula to manage your teen's behaviour challenges. Parents have often asked me for a specific way of managing problems as they crop up. This reveals the greatest secret which is going to make your parenting effective. This simple to use formula can solve any problem.

Secret No. 101

Impart Positivity Consistently: The key to helping teens thrive lies in imparting positivity consistently. Encourage daily habits like gratitude journaling or reflection on wins, big or small. These simple routines build resilience and a growth mindset, empowering teens to turn challenges into opportunities for growth.